CORPORATE ENVIRONMENTAL RESPONSIBILITY IN THE HYDRO-ELECTRICITY AND WATER SECTORS IN CAMEROON: A LEGAL PERSPECTIVE

Bibliografische Information der Deutschen Nationalbibliothek
Die Deutsche Nationalbibliothek verzeichnet diese Publikation in der Deutschen Nationalbibliografie; detaillierte bibliografische Daten sind im Internet über http://dnb.ddb.de abrufbar.

Direct all inquiries to Galda Verlag, Franz-Schubert-Str. 61, 16548 Glienicke, Germany

ISBN 978-3-96203-131-2 (Print)
ISBN 978-3-96203-132-9 (E-Book)

CORPORATE ENVIRONMENTAL RESPONSIBILITY IN THE HYDRO-ELECTRICITY AND WATER SECTORS IN CAMEROON: A LEGAL PERSPECTIVE

ROLAND DJIEUFACK
MBIFI RICHARD
CYPRIAN MBOU MONOJI

DEDICATION

To our parents

PREFACE

This book has its origin in independent contributions made by the various authors owing much to the wisdom and acquired knowledge on these subjects drawn from independent research. As a collaborative venture, it has been a stimulating and enjoyable experience.

Our ambition has been to write a book which sets out to make a briliant insight into some specific issues underlying principles and structure of energy and water laws in Cameroon. Energy and water laws have been subject to numerous significant developments and have undergone some important legislative changes with the rapid trend of indsutrialisation and globalisation in Cameroon. This has been taking place within an increasingly liberalised market place in which the global drive to compete brings new challenges to regulatory authorities and a corresponding impact on consumers' behaviour.

The primary objective of this book therefore is to examine critically the environmental aspects of corporate social responsibility in the utility service sector namely; hydro-electricity and water sectors in Cameroon and how that connects to governmental policy. ENEO and CamWater who are respectively the unique hydro-electrical and water corporations in Cameroon are recognised as an impetus to economic, social, cultural and political advancement. Surprisingly, in this strive to achieve economic development, little or no consideration has been given to environmental effects of their activities even when government's principal responsibility has been to ensure social and environmental safety as well as mitigate any damage. Even when social and environmental problems have arisen, they have been minimised "in the public interest". As a result, corporate environmental policies have not occupied a priority position on the agenda of these corporate bodies and its implementation as such is relatively slow. The outcome of this has been the perpetration of corporate conduct that is negligent of safeguards that mitigate environmental degradation even when the State has taken measures through legislations to set social and environmental standards in a bid to regulate corporate conducts that contribute to environmental safety to the local communities. While acknowledging the innovations in these laws, we equally argue that this has taken place within the ambit of weak and insufficiently articulated policies. Sanctions and implementation have not been stringent enough to effectively deter these utility service providers from violating corporate environmental responsibility as corroborated by the increase in the number of cases on violation of this responsibility.

The improtance of hydro-electricity and water laws should not be underestimated as they are not just law subjects for lawyers. At one level, it can serve as an introduction for students in that there is not too much information on any one topic. But we hope that, at another level, the work will merit the attention of shcolars, legal practioners, enrionmentalists, businessmen, human rights activists and the government. The views expressed may be controversial in parts, but they aim to be a contribution to scholarly debate on the analysis of corporate environmental governance within the hydro-electricity and water sectors in Cameroon.

We would like to thank a number of individuals and structures for their very helpful comments, support and patience. In particular, our thanks are due to some indigenes found in the Edea and Songloubouhydro-electricity generation plants in Cameroon. We equally thank those persons living within the Bamenda, Buea, Douala, Dschang and Limbe municipalities of Cameroon who fed us with water related problems. We also owe a debt of gratitude to some government structures particuarly the Ministry of Energy and Water Resources.

We take all excuses for any errors or omissions that we may have made.

Roland Djieufack, Ph.D
Richard Mbifi, Ph.D
Cyprian Mbou Monoji, Ph. D
25 May 2020
Bamenda, Cameroon

FOREWORD

This intellectual masterpiece has as objective to shed light in 'dark' areas of contemporary energy and water laws in Cameroon. A book on the corporate environmental governance of some utility services namely, the hydroelectricity and water sectors in Cameroon (an area of natural resource law not adequately researched on) has been very timely unveiled. It is justified for addressing the environmental aspects of corporate social responsibility of companies within the hydroelectricity and water sectors in Cameroon and so merits its place in contemporary discuss.

The authors' timely publication coincides with an era of mounting and incessant complaints from local communities relating to the diminutive attention given to environmental and human right concerns by the National Electricity Corporation (ENEO) and the Water Corporation (Cam Water) in their respective domains where they have implanted their equipment and generation plants. The book is therefore a distillation of ideas that have undergone a long period of germination and have been garnered from a wide range of sources. This book reveals not only the complex arrangements that exist in private and public laws governing electricity and water transactions but also unveils the implicit concerns of geographic and environmental sciences.

The authors carefully reiterate the respect of environmental norms by advocating for the fact that these utility service providers are bound to take responsibility for any environmental damage that are contrary to existing environmental norms. In this book, the authors have carefully discussed their viewpoints from a legal perspective. They have drawn from existing literature on electricity and water laws in general in Cameroon, analysed the relevant national and international statutes and elucidated on materials drawn from extensive field experiences in Cameroon.

The book is written in five chapters. Chapter One opens with a general introduction. The second chapter highlights the relevant national and international regulatory frameworks on electricity and water in Cameroon. Chapter three examines the need for environmental governance in the Cameroonian economy. The fourth chapter investigates on the effective compliance and enforcement mechanisms of existing laws affecting the hydro-electricity and water sectors by these corporations, while the fifth dwells on the offences and sanctions for violating environmental responsibility in Cameroon. The succinct and coherent layout of the chapters provides the reader with an appetite to peruse the major themes in their entirety. The publication is written in an engaging and simple style that entices the curiosity of prospective readers.

I have no doubt, therefore, that Cameroon's natural resource laws specifically relating to harnessing its water resources and energy supply will rise to these expectations in this realm of technological advancements and huge investment projects. I strongly salute these young and enthusiastic authors for their interest in this portentous area of the law where they have proffered a blend of theory and practice. Certainly, this will address the legitimate needs of the local populace in Cameroon in the medium and long-run.

FOMBE Lawrence, (Ph.D.)
Professor of Development Studies and Regional Planning
Director, Higher Institute of Transport and Logistics
The University of Bamenda, Cameroon

TABLE OF CONTENTS

TABLE OF STATUTES

National Statutes

Laws

- The 1972 Constitution of the Republic of Cameroon.
- Law No. 64/LF/3 of April 1964 Governing Mineral Substances.
- Law No. 65/LF/24 of 12 November 1965 and Law No 67/LF/1 of 12 June 1967 on the Penal Code.
- Law No. 74/23 of 5th April 1974 on the Organisation of Councils.
- Law No. 78/24 of December 1978 Fixing the Fiscal Regime for Collecting Mining Revenue.
- Law No. 86/008 of 5 July 1986 on Gas and Water Vapour Pressure Equipment.
- Law No. 89/027 of 27 December 1989 on Toxic Waste.
- Law No. 89/027 of 29 December 1989, Banning the Introduction, Stockage, Detention, Transportation, Transit and Deposit on the National Territory of Toxic and or Dangerous Wastes in all forms.
- Law No. 90/53 of 19 December 1990 on the Freedom of Association.
- Law No. 92/007 of 14 August 1992 on the Cameroon Labour Code.
- Law No. 93/004 of 16 July 1993, to ratify the Bamako Convention on the Ban of the Import into Africa and the Control of Trans-boundary Movement and Management of Hazardous Waste within Africa 1991.
- Law No 93/010 of 22 December 1993, to ratify the UN Framework Convention on Climate Change 1992.
- Law No. 94/01 of 20 January 1994 to lay down Forestry, Wildlife and Fisheries Regulations.
- Law No. 95/20 of 8 August 1995, to ratify the United Nations Convention to Combat Desertification 1994.
- Law No. 96/06 of 18 January 1996 on the Constitution of Cameroon.

- Law No. 96/06 of 18 January 1996 on the Constitution of Cameroon.
- Law No. 96/12 of 5th August 1996 relating to Environmental Management in Cameroon.
- Law No. 98/005 of 14 April1998 to lay down the Water Code.
- Law No. 99/013 of 22 December 1999, Relating to the Petroleum Code.
- Law No. 99/14 of 22 December 1999, Relating to Non-Governmental Organisations in Cameroon.
- Law No. 001/2001 of 16 April 2001, instituting the Mining Code.
- Law No. 2002/013 of 30th December 2002 to Institute the Gas Code.
- Law No. 2002/013 of 30th December 2002 to Institute the Gas Code as modified by Law No. 2012/006 of the 19th April 2012.
- Law No. 2004/18 of 22nd July 2004 laying down the Rules Applicable to Councils.
- Law No 2005/003 of 28 April 2005 to ratify the Stockholm Convention on Persistent Organic Pollutant 2001.
- Law No. 2006/015 of 29 December 2006 on Judicial Organisation of Court in Cameroon.
- Law No. 2009/001 of 14 April 2009, to ratify the Montreal Protocol on Substances that Deplete the Ozone Layer, 1987 and its amendment of 1997.
- Law No. 2011/022 of 14 December 2011 governing the Electricity sector in Cameroon.
- Law No. 2011/012 of 6 May 2011 on Consumer Protection in Cameroon.
- Law No. 2011/027, of 14 December 2011 amending certain provisions of Law No. 2006/015 of 29 December 2006 on Judicial Organisation of Court.
- Law No. 2012/006 of 19 April 2012 to Institute the Gas Code.
- Law No. 2016/007 of July 12 2016, relating to the Penal Code.

Decrees and Orders

- Decree No.76/372 of 2 September 1976 to Regulate Establishments Classified as Dangerous, Unhygienic and Obnoxious.

- Decree No. 84/797 of 17 July 1984 Organising the then Ministry of Planning and Territorial Administration.
- Decree No. 92/069 of 9 April 1992 on the Creation of the Ministry of Environment and Forestry (MINEF).
- Decree No. 94/259/PM of 31st May 1994 relating to the Organisation and Functioning of the National Consultative Commission on the Environment and Sustainable Development.
- Decree No 95/466/PM, of 20th July 1995 to lay down Conditions for the Implementation of Wildlife.
- Decree No95/531 of August 1995 on the Implementation of the Forestry Law.
- Decree No. 96/24 of 01 October 1996 Reorganising the Ministry of Environment and Forestry.
- Decree No. 99/780/PM of 11 October 1999 Modifying and Completing the Provisions of Article 3(1) of Decree N0 94/259/PM of 31 May 1994 on the Creation of a National Consultative Commission for Environment and Sustainable Development.
- Decree No. 2000/485 of 30 June 2000 on the Modalities of the Application of the Petroleum Code.
- Decree No. 2001/163/PM of 8 May 2001 regulating the Perimeter of Protection of the Sources of Water and Treatment of Water Stored for Portable Use.
- Decree No. 2001/164/PM of 8th May 2001 Regulating the Utilization of Water Resources.
- Decree No. 2001/165/PM of 8th May 2001, on the Protection of Water Resources.
- Decree No. 2001/718/PM of 03 September 2001 relating to the Organisation and Functioning of the Inter-Ministerial Committee on Environment.
- Decree No. 2002/216 of 21st August, 2002 on the Reorganisation of the Government.
- Decree No. 2002/648/PM du 26 Mars 2002 fixing the Modalities for the Application of Law No. 001/2001 of 16 April 2001 Instituting the Mining Code.

- Decree No. 2003/2034/PM of 4th September 2003 to lay down the Terms and Conditions for the Implementation of the Gas Code.
- Decree No 2004/320 of 8th December 2004, Organising the Government.
- Decree No. 2005/087 of 29 March 2005 on the Organisation of the Ministry of Water and Energy.
- Decree No. 2005/118 of 15 April 2005, on the Organisation of the Ministry of Agriculture and Rural Development.
- Decree No 95/466/PM, of 20th July 1995 to lay down Conditions for the Implementation of Wildlife.
- Decree No 95/531/PM, of 23 July 1995 to lay down Conditions for the Procedure for Implementing the Forestry Law.
- Decree No.2005/0577/PM of 23 February 2005, fixing the Modalities for Environmental Impact Assessment.
- Decree No. 2011/2585/PM of August 2011, fixing the list of Harmful or Dangerous Substances and the Regime of their Discharge into Continental Waters.
- Decree No. 2012/431 of 1st October 2012, on the Organisation of the Ministry of Environment, Nature Protection and Sustainable Development.
- Decree No. 2012/432 of 1st October 2012, on the Organization of the Ministry of Mines, Industry and Technological Development.
- Order No.0070/MINEP of 22 April 1970 to fix the Different Categories of Projects Submitted to Environmental Impact Assessment.
- Order No. 13 of 19 April 1977, Naming Classified Factories.
- Notice No. D69/NC/MSP/DMPH/SHPA of August 1980 relating to the Collection, the Transportation and Treatment of Industrial Waste, Domestic Waste Treatment Plants and Sanitary Sewage Matters.
- Order No. 0069/MINEP of March 2005 on the Different Categories of Projects that would necessitate an Environmental Impact Assessment.
- Order No. 0070/MINEP of 22 April 2005, fixing the different category of projects whose oneribes is submitted to Environmental Impact Assessment.

International Statutes

- United Nations Charter 1945.
- American Declaration on Human Rights and Duties of Man 1948
- European Convention for the Protection of Human Rights and Fundamental Freedoms 1950.
- International Covenant on Civil and Political Rights 1966.
- Stockholm Declaration of June 16 1972.
- African Charter on Human and Peoples Rights (ACHPR) 1981.
- Vienna Convention on the Protection of the Ozone Layer, 1985.
- Montreal Protocol on Substances that Deplete the Ozone Layer, 1987.
- Bamako Convention on the Ban of the Import into Africa and the Control of Trans-boundary Movement and Management of Hazardous Wastes within Africa, 1991.
- United Nations Framework Convention on Climate Change, 1992.
- Agenda 21, of the 1992 Rio Earth Summit.
- Basel Convention on the Control of Trans-boundary Movements of Hazardous Wastes and their Disposal, 1992.
- Rio de Janeiro Conference in 1992.
- OHADA Uniform Act on General Commercial Law.
- OHADA Uniform Act on Economic Groupings and Interest Groups.
- OHADA Accounting Law.
- United Nations Framework Convention on Climate Change 1992.
- United Nations Convention to Combat Desertification, 1994.
- Stockholm Convention on Persistent Organic Pollutant, 2001.
- International Covenant on Economic, Social and Cultural Rights (ICESPR)
- Stockholm Convention on Persistent Organic Pollutants, 2004.

TABLE OF CASES

Local Cases

- *ALUCAM Co Ltd v MINEF*, No. 10/PVA/MINEF/BP/EF/SPE of 21 March 2001. (unreported)
- Affaire Ministère Public et Ministre d'Environnement et de forets c/ Sadou Mana, BowanaRoul, Nana Augustine, HaouaBolade, judgément No. 568/COR du 06 Janvier 1998. (unreported)
- *ComplexeCosmétique de l'Ouest (CCO) v. MINEF*, No. 004/PVI/MINEF/DPEF/SPE of 15 January 2002. (unreported)
- *DRAGAGE DTP v MINEF*, No. 070/MINEF/SPE/DNIE 2001 (unreported)
- *Foundation for Environment (FEDEV) v. China Road and Bridge Corporation* CFIB/004M/09
- *Foundation for Environment (FEDEV) v. BAMENDA URBAN COUNCIL*, HCB/117M/04-05
- *KETCHSCEMAR v. MINEF*, No. 060/MINEF/SPE/DNIE of January 2001 (Unreported)
- *KETCH v. MINEP*, No. 94/PVA/MINEP/DPE/FCE/SPE of June 2002. (Unreported)
- *MINEF v. Cameroon Railway Corporation (CAMRAIL)*, Case No. 20/TPI/DLA, 12 April 2003. (Unreported)
- *MINEP v. SOFAMAC*, No. 008/12/PVCI/MINEP/SG/DNC/BIE. (Unreported)
- *MINEP v. AZA INC. AFRIGAZ*, No. 110/N/MINEP/SG/DNC/BIE/SG, 11/08/09. (Unreported)
- *MINEP v. SociétéAluminium du Cameroun (ALUCAM)*, No. 028/NA/20/MINEP/DRLT/BRIE, 22/10/10. (Unreported)

- *MINEP v. AES-SONEL*, No. 0017/N/MINEP/SG/DNC/BIE/USC/CEAI, 13/04/11. (Unreported)
- *MINEPDED v. Société Transformation REEF Cameroun (TRC), Scierie de Kumba*, No. 056/PVCI/MINEPDED/SG/DRO/BRIE-of 07/12/2011. (Unreported)
- *MINEPDED v. Union Trade International (UTI) Douala*, No. 84/PVCI/11/MINEPDED/DRLT/BRIE/of 15/12/2011. (Unreported)
- *MINEP v. OMNIUM SERVICE Douala*, No. 85/PVCI/11/MINEP/DRLT/BRIE/of 19/12/2011. (Unreported)
- *MINEP v. PLACAM*, No. 01/PVCI/MINEP/SG/DNC//BIE, 20/04/2012
- *MINEPDED v. African Distilling Company (ADIC)*, No. 01/2012/PVCI/MINEPDED/DRCE/DDHS of 07/03/2012, (Unreported).
- *MINEP v SOFAMAC*, No. 07/MINEP/EPE/DNIEBEIE/C4 of 17 November 2005 (Unreported)
- *MINEP v. CDE AgenceAdamaoua*, No. 001/PVCI/MINEP/SG/DNC/BIE of 19/04/2012. (Unreported)
- *MINEPDED v. Station Service Cameroon Oil Company (CAMOCO) Ngaoundere*, No.0002/PVCI/MINEPDED/DRAD/BIE of 14/02/2012. (Unreported)
- *MINEPDED v. Depot Guinness de Ngaoundere-Baladji 2 (Depot de Transit)*, No.001/PVCI/RADD/DREPDED of 27/03/2012. (Unreported)
- *MINEPDED v. Station Service OilibyaGare, Ngaoundere*, No. 0006/PVCI/MINEPDED/DRAD/BIE of 26/02/2012. (Unreported)
- *MINEPDED v. Station Service MSR Grand Marche, Ngaoundere*, No. 0005/PVCI/MINEPDED/DRAD/BIE of 16/02/2012. (Unreported)
- *MINEPDED v. Station Service MSR Aeroport, Ngaoundere*, No. 0009/PVCI/MINEPDED/DRAD/BIE of 21/02/2012. (Unreported)
- *MINEPDED v. Station Service TOTAL, Depot de Ngaoundere S/C EtablissementMohamadouBachirou*, No.0007/PVCI/MINEPDED/DRAD/BIE of 21/02/2012. (Unreported)
- *MINEPDED v. Station Service TOTAL, centre de Ngaoundere*, No. 0001/PVCI/MINEPDED/DRAD/BIE of 14/02/2012. (Unreported)

- *MINEPDED v. Station Service TOTAL, Route Garoua*, No.0008/PVCI/MINEPDED/DRAD/BIE of 21/02/2012. (Unreported)
- *MINEPDED v. Etablissement SOTONG (Station Service Total Akonolinga*, No. 030/12/PVCI/MINEPDED/DRCE/BIE of22/02/2012. (Unreported)
- *MINEPDED v. African Distilling Company (ADIC), Usine de Mbandjock*, No. 01/2012/PVCI/MINEPDED/DRCE/DDHS of 07/03/2012. (Unreported)
- *MINEPDED v. Complex Industriel du Centre (CIC), Yaoundé*, No. 052/12/PVCI/MINEPDED/DRCE/BIE of 12/04/2012. (Unreported)
- *MINEPDED v. Société BUNS, Carrièred'Oyack 1 Mbalmayo, Yaoundé*, No. 015/12/PVCI/MINEPDED/DNC/BIE of 24/04/2012. (Unreported)
- *MINEPDED v. Centre d'Etude des Travaux Publics, Chantier de Dschang*, No. 34/PVCI/MINEPDED/DRO/DD/DDM of 24/02/2012. (Unreported)
- *MINEPDED v. AQUARREL, Nomayos – Yaoundé*, No. 06/12/PVCI/MINEPDED/DRCE/DDMAK of 14/05/2012. (Unreported)
- *MINEPDEDv. CAMINCO, GarouaBoulai*, No. 002/PVCI/MINEPDED/SG/DRE/BRIE/LD of 01/06/2012. (Unreported)
- *MINEPDED v. CFC NGOLLA*, No. 005/PVCI/MINEPDED/DRE/BRIE/ of 03/05/2012. (Unreported)
- *MINEP v. La Société AES SONEL (Centre thermique de Tibati)*, No. 002/PVCI/MINEP/SG/DNC/BIE of 25/04/2012. (Unreported)
- *MINEP v. FokouFoberdNgaoundere, (Installation du Quartier Zimbabwe, Ngaoundere)*, No. 003/PVCI/MINEP/SG/DNC/BIE of 27/04/2012. (Unreported)
- *MINEP v. AES SONEL (Centralethermique de Ngaoundal)*, No. 004/PVCI/MINEP/SG/DNC/BIE of 27/04/2012. (Unreported)
- *MINEP v. Société SOUBIE MAG SARL (Carrière de pierres de Tibati Djerem)*, No. 009/PVCI/RAD/DREPDED/BIE of 25/04/2012. (Unreported)
- *MINEP v. BOCOM Tibati*, No. 011/PVCI/RAD/DREPED/BIE of 05/07/2012. (Unreported)

- *MINEP v. PLACAM Yaoundé*, No. 01/PVCI/MINEP/SG/DNC/BIE of 23/04/2012. (Unreported)
- *MINEP v. SOLET Douala*, No. 02/PVCI/MINEP/SG/DNC/BIE of 25/04/2012. (Unreported)
- *MINEP v. Société ESTNO SARL* Douala, No. 03/PVCI/MNEP/SG/DNC/BIE of 27/04/2012. (Unreported)
- *MINEP v. Compagnie Industrielle du sud (CIS)-Douala*, No.93/PVCI/12/MINEP/DRLT/BRIE of 25/01/2012. (Unreported)
- *MINEP v. Atlantis Plastics Douala*, No. 0005/PVCI/MINEP/SG/DNC/BIE of 23/04/2012. (Unreported)
- *MINEP v. LaboratoiresBiopharma S.A Douala*, No. 0005/PVCI/MINEP/SG/DNC/BIE of 23/04/2012. (Unreported)
- *MINEP v. ChocolaterieetConfiseries du Cameroon (CHOCOCAM) Douala*, No. 04/03/04/12/PVCI/MINEP/SG/DNC/BIE of 23/04/2012. (Unreported)
- *MINEP v. Complexe Industriel d'Afrique Cenrale, Douala*, No. 01//03/04/12/PVCI/MINEP/SG/DNC/BIE of 19/04/2012. (Unreported)..............319
- *MINEP v. FERMENCAM*, No. 002/PVCI/MINEP/SG/DNC/BIE of 25/04/2012. (Unreported)
- *MINEP v. AES-SONEL (Magasin de Bassa) Douala*, No. PVCI/MINEP/SG/DNC/BIE/of 24/04/2012. (Unreported)
- *MINEP v. AES-SONEL (Post TransformateurBekoko)-Douala*, No. 007/PVCI/MINEP/SG/DNC/BIE/of 03/05/2012. (Unreported)
- *MINEP v. SIC CACAOS Douala*, No. 008/PVCI/MINEP/SG/DNC/BIE/of 03/05/2012. (Unreported)
- *MINEP v. Société de Développement du Coton (SODECOTON) Huilerie, Egrenage, Garage et Décharge Garoua*, matter No. 04/PVCI/MINEP/SG/DNC/BIE/DRN/DDB of 03/05/2012. (Unreported)
- *MINEP v. AES SONEL (Centrale thermique de poli) Douala*, No. 08/PVCI/MINEP/SG/DNC/BIE/DRN/DDB of 07/05/2012. (Unreported)
- *MINEP v. Ndu Tea Plantation*, No. 002/NO/PVCI/MINEP/SG/DNC/BIE of 20/04/2012. (Unreported)

- *MINEP v. International Soap Factory Company Limited – Bamenda*, No. 001/NO/PVCI/MINEP/SG/DNC/BIE of 18/04/2012. (Unreported)
- *MINEPDED v. OILIBYA – Mbouda*, No. 002/PVCI/MINEPDED/SG/DRO/BRIE of 8/08/2012. (Unreported)
- MINEP v. AES SONEL (Centralethermiqued'Ambam)-Douala, matter No. 01/SUD/PVCI/MINEP/SG/DNC/BIE of 17/04/2012. (Unreported)
- *MINEP v. CTE, ToleBuea*, No. 04/L/MINEP/PDSW/BIE/SW/2012 of 02/02/2012. (Unreported)
- *MINEPDED v. SCIERIE WUMA/CAFECO*, Nguti, No. 01/PVCI/MINEPDED/SG/DNC/BIE of 09/12/2012. (Unreported)
- *MINEPDED v. Etablissements EXTECHOCAM Tiko*, No. 039/ON/MINEPDED/ SWR/RDEPDED/F/DDEDPDED/12 of 20/02/2012. (Unreported)
- *MINEPDED v. La SociétéCongelcamLimbe*, No. 038/ON/MINEPDED/SWR/RDEPDED/F/DDEDPDED/12 of 27/02/2012. (Unreported)
- *MINEPDED v. La Camerounaise Des Eaux (CDE)*, No. 035/ON/MINEPDED/SWR/RDEPDED/F/DDEDPDED/12 of 17/02/2012. (Unreported)
- *MINEPDED v. Station Service CORLAY MRS Mile 17 Buea*, No.072/I/MINEPDED/SWR/RDEPDED/F/DDEDPDED/12 of 07/02/2012. (Unreported)
- *MINEP v. Station Service CORLAY MRS Muyuka*, No. 029/ON/MINEP/RDEP/SWR/DDEP/F/12 of 24/01/2012. (Unreported)
- *MINEPDEDv. MuyukaAgro IndustrialFarm*, No.035/ON/MINEPDED/SWR/RDEPDED/F/DDEDPDED/12 of 17/02/2012. (Unreported)
- *MINEPDED v. Station Service TOTAL Limbe*, No. 035/ON/MINEPDED/ SWR/RDEPDED/F/DDEDPDED/12 of 28/03/2012. (Unreported)
- *MINEP v. Société Industrielle de Transformation de Ble*, No. 002/PVCI/MINEP/SG/DNC/BIE-of 26/04/2012. (Unreported)
- *MINEP v. Union Camerounaise des Brasseries (UCB) Douala*, No. 002/PVCI/MINEP/SG/DNC/BIE/of 19/04/2012. (Unreported)

- *MINEPDED v. Capitaine de Navire MV LADY ROSE, S/C SOCOPAO (Bollore Africa Logistics Cameroon)* Douala, No. 99/PVCI/MINEPDED/SG/DRO/BRIE of 19/04/2012. (Unreported)
- *MINEPDED v. Brasserie du Cameroun (centre de Distribution d'Ombe)*, No. 035/ON/MINEPDED/SWR/RDEPDED/F/DDEDPDED/12 of 09/07/2012. (Unreported)
- *MINEP v. TRANSITALLA*, No. 107/PVCI/11/MINEP/DRLT/BRIE/of 07/08/2012. (Unreported)
- MINEPDED v. SOCAMIT OIL Douala, No. 05/PVCI/MINEPDED/DRLT/DD-MI/SIEE/of 18/09/2012. (Unreported)
- *MINEPDED v. FOMA INTERPRISER Douala*, No. 95/PVCI/11/MINEPDED/DRLT/BRIE of 15/02/2012. (Unreported)
- *MINEPDED v. CAMTRADE BURREAU SA Douala*, No. 96/PVCI/11/MINEPDED/DRLT/BRIE of 09/03/2012. (Unreported)
- *SCAN EQUIP v. MINEP*, Case No. 90/TPI/DLA/March 2002 (Unreported)
- *SOTRAMILK v MINEF*, Case No. 08/CF/BA/1245/02.03 (Unreported)
- *SOSUCAM BANJOCK v MINEP*, No. 010/12/PVCI/MINEP/SG/DNC/BIE OF 23 April 2012. (Unreported)
- *SOSUCAM NKOTENG v MINEP*, No. 011/12/PVCI/MINEP/SG/DNC/BIE of 23 April 2012. (Unreported)
- *Station Service TOTAL Moyuka v NINEPDED*, No. 51/I/MINEP/RDEP/SWR/DDEP/11 of 10 November 2011. (Unreported)
- *Station Service TOTAL II Limbe v MINEPDED*, No. 036/ON/MINEPDED/SWR/RDEPDED/F/DDED/PDED/12 of 21 February 2012. (Unreported)
- *Station Service TRADEX Limbe v. MINEPDED*, No. 049/ON/MINEPDED/SWR/RDEPDED/F/DDEP/DED/12 of 10 July 2012. (Unreported).
- *The People (MINEF) V. Tame Soumedjong and SOTRAMILK (LTD)*, Case No. CFIBA/857C/02-03. (Unreported).
- *The People of Cameroon v. Bissong Daniel Nkwo Alias Bukande.*(2004), CFING/107c/03-04 (Unreported).

- *The People (MINEF) v. Bertrand Brink and Groupement Coop BUNS* CFIB/87C/03-04 .
- *The People of Cameroon (MINEF) v Tonye, Nken*, Reference No. 005/ PVCI/MINEF/DPEFC/SPFAP/ 27/02/03. (Unreported).
- *United Transport Africa (UTA) Cameroon SA v. MINEP*, No. 07/pv/ MINEP/SG/SPE/DNIE of 23rd February 2004 (Unreported).

Foreign Cases

- *7up v. Abiola*, [2001] 5 M.J.S.C 93
- *A.I.E. v. Adebayo* [2003] 12 M.J.S.C 44
- *Abakaliki Local Government Council v. Abakaliki Rice Mills Owners Enterprises Nigeria* (1990) 6 N.W.L.R. (pt. 155) 182
- *Abu v. Odugbo*, [2001] 7 M.J.S.C 87
- *Adeshina v. Lemour* (1965) 1 All N.L.R. 233
- *A-G Adamawa State v. A-G Federation* [2006] I M.J.S.C 1
- *A-G Federation v. A-G of the 36 States* [2001] 6M J.S.C 69
- *Akibu v. Azeez*, (2003) 5 N.W.L.R. (Pt. 814) 643
- *Amadi v. N.N.P.C* (2000) 10 N.W.L.R (Pt. 674) 6
- *Amos v. Shell B.P. Nigeria Limited* (1974) 4 E.C.S.L.R 486
- *Arabambi v. A.B.I. Ltd* [2006]3 M.J.S.C 61
- *Aremo11 v. Adekanye*, [2004] 11 M.J.S.C 11
- *Asogwa v. Chukwu*, (2003) 4 N.W.L.R (pt. 811) 540
- *Auckland City Council v North Power Ltd* [2004] NZRMA 354
- *Auckland Regional Council v Times Media Ltd* (District Court, Auckland, CRN 2084004885, 16 June 2003, McElrea DCJ)
- *Axer Pty Ltd v Environment Protection Authority*, (1993), 113 LGERA 357 at 359-360
- *Bentley v. BGP Properties Pty Ltd* [2006] N.S.W.L.E.C. 34 (6 February 2006) at [145], [149]
- *Brimble v, Epping Rubber Company Pty Ltd* [1990] N.S.W.L.E.C. 94 (17 August 1990)
- *Burnie Port Authority v. General Jones Pty. Ltd.* (1994) 68 A.L.R. 331 (Austl.)

- *Cambridge Water Co. v. Eastern Counties Leather PLC*, 1 All E.R. 53 (H.L. 1994)
- Case of *Langforth 79 Eng*. Rep. 919 (K.B. 1635)
- Case of *Metalclad v United Mexican States*, ICSID case No. ARB(AF)/97/1 (ICSIDAF) August 30, 2000
- *Corfu Channel* case, case between *United Kingdom v. Albania*, Merits, 1949 I.C.J. Rep. 4, 22-23 (Judgement of April 9).
- *Dr.MohinddinFarooque v. Bangladesh and others*, CA. No. 24, 1995
- *Edjerode v. Ikine* [2002]2 M.J.S.C 163
- *Ejem v. Offiah* (2000) 7 N.W.L.R (pt. 666) 662
- *ELF Nigeria limited v. Sillo&Anor* (1994) 6 N.W.L.R (pt. 350) 258
- *Environment Protection Authority v Gardner* [1997] NSWLEC 212 (7 November 1997)
- *Environment Protection Authority v HochtiefAG* [2006] NSWLEC 200 (28 April 2006) at [99]
- *Environment Protection Authority v Incitec Ltd* [2003] NSWLEC 381 (1 October 2003) at [61]
- *Environmental Protection Authority v. Waste Recycling and Processing Corporation* [2006] N.S.W.L.E.C. 419 (10 July 2006) at [226]
- *Eze v. A-G Rivers State* [2002] 1 M.J.S.C 87
- *Eze v. Okechukwu* (2003) 02 M.J.S.C. 188
- *Factory of Chorzor case, Case between Germany vs. Poland* PCJI, (1928), Ser. A, no. 17, p. 29
- *GaniFawehinwi v. Central Bank of Nigeria and 4Ors*. Case No. FHL/L/CS/53/92
- *Gittany Constructions Pty Limited v Sutherland Shire Council* [2006] NSWLEC 242 (10 May 2006) at [193]
- *Green Peace v. E. C. Commission* 1998 EVR
- *Inkson v. R* (1996) 88 A. Crim. R. 334 at 345
- *IRC v. National Federation of Self-Employed and Small Business Ltd*, 1982 AC 617
- *Jika v. Akuson* (2006) ALL FWLR (pt.293)

- Lac Lanoux Abitration, (*Spain v. France*) XII R.I.A.A. 281 (1957)
- *Lopez Ostra vs. Spain*, 20 E.H.R.R. 277
- *Machinery Movers Ltd v Auckland Regional Council* [1994] 1 NZLR 492 at 503…187
- *MainaKamanda&Anor. V. Nairobi City Council &Anor* HCCC No. 5403 of 1989
- *Mehta v. Union of India AIR* (1968) SL 155
- *Menakaya v. Menakaya* [2001] 8 M.J.S.C 50
- *Mobil Producing (Nigeria)Unlimited v. LASEPA* (2002) M.J.S.C 69
- *Ndule v. Ibezim* [2002] 12 M.J.S.C 150
- *Nigeria Cement Co. Ltd v. Nigeria Railway Corporation &Anor* (1992) 1 N.W.L.R (Pt. 22) 747
- *Nigerian Ports Plc V. Oseni* (2000) 8 N.W.L.R (Pt. 669) 410
- *Okolo v. U.B.N*, [2004] 2 M.J.S.C 69
- *People v. Corporation of Albany*, 11 Wend. 539, 543 (N. Y. Sup. Ct. 1834)
- *Piva v Brinkworth*, (1992) 59 SASR 92 at 96
- *Queen v. Birmingham & Gloucester Ry.*, 114 Eng. Rep. 492 (Q.B. 1842)
- *Queen v. Stephens*, L.R.1 Q.B. 702 (1866)
- *R v Bata Industries Ltd* (1992) 9 OR (3d) 329, 7 CELR (NS) 245 at [184]
- *R v City of Sault Ste Marie* [1978] 2 SCR 1299; 85 DLR (3d) 161 at 172 [28]
- *R v Leung* (1999) 48 NSWLR 340 at 363 [127]
- *R v Newman* (2004) 145 A Crim R 361 at [82]
- *R v Palu* (2002) 134 A Crim R 174 at 183-184 [37]
- *R v Rushby* [1977] 1 NSWLR 594 at 597-598
- *R v Sharp* (2004) 142 A Crim R 140 at [35]
- *R v Simpson* (2004) 145 A Crim R 361 at [82]
- *R v Slack* [2004] NSWCCA 128 (7 May 2004) at [60]
- *R v Walsh*, (2004) 142 A Crim R 140 at [35]
- *R v Wilson* [2005] NSWCCA 219 (17 June 2005) at [26]

- *R v Wong* (1999) 48 NSWLR 340 at 363 [127]
- *R v, Anglican Water Services Ltd* [204] 1 Cr. App. R. (S) 62, [2004] J.P.L. 458 at [12], [14]
- *R v. Geddes* (1936) 36 SR (NSW) 554 at 555; (1936) 53 WN (NSW) 157 at 158
- *R v. Nichols* (1991) 57 A. Crim. R. 391 at 395
- *R v. United Keno Mines Ltd* (1980) 1 Y.R. 299; 10 C.E.L.R. 43 at (9)
- *Ryland v Fletcher*. LR, 3H.L330; 1868
- *Selwyn Mews Ltd v Auckland City Council* (High Court of New Zealand, Auckland, CRI-2003-404-159- 161, 30 April 2004, Randerson J) at [36]
- *Senator Adesanya v. President of Nigeria* (1981) 2 N.C.L.R 388
- *Shanks &Mc Ewan (Teeside) Ltd v. Environment Agency*
- *Shell Petroleum Development Company Nigeria Limited v. Chief Otoko&Ors*. (1990) 6 N.W.L.R (pt 159) 693
- *Sken Consult v. Ukey* (1981) 1 S.C. 6
- *Southern Bluefin Tuna* Case, Case between *Australia and New Zealand v. Japan*. On 27 August 1999
- *Teno Engineering Ltd v. Adisa*, (2003) 4 N.W.L.R (pt. 811) 540
- *The Attoney General Legos State v. The Hon*, (1989) ANLR, 504, p.511-51
- *Thomas v. Olufosoye (1985) 3NWLR (pt 13)523*
- *Trial Smelter* Arbitration case between the *United States of America v. Canada*
- *University of Ife v. FawehinmiConstruction Co. Ltd* (1991) 7 N.W.L.R (pt. 201) 26
- *Van Melike v. Costa Aerosa* 1975 (1) SA 225
- *Veen v. R* (No. 2) (1988) 164 C.L.R. 465, 476
- *Verstappen v. Port Edward Town Board and Others* (1994) (3) SA 569) D
- *Waikato Regional Council v Huntly Quarries Ltd* (District Court, Auckland, CRN 2024011394, 30 October 2003), McElrea DCJ)
- *Walker v Eves*, (1976) 13 SASR 249 at 250
- *WangariMaathai v. Kenya Times Media Trust*, HCCC No. 5403 of 1989

- *Waste Management Inc v United Mexican States*, (ICSID), case No.ARB(AF)98/2 June 2, 2000
- *Yahaya v. The State* (2002) 3 M.J.S.C 103
- *Yesufu v. Governor Edo State* [2001] 5m.J.S.C 128

ABBREVIATIONS

ACHPR	African Charter on Human and Peoples' Rights
API	l'Agence de Promotion des Investissement
AU	African Union
BSR	Business for Social Responsibility
CAPME	Centre for the Promotion of and Assistance to Small and Medium-sized enterprises
CBD	Convention on Biological Diversity
CCIMA	Chambre de Commerce, d'Industrie, des Mines et de l'Artisanat
CDB	Cameroon Development Bank
CDE	Camerounais des Eaux
CEMAC	Central African Economic and Monetary Community
CH4	Methane
CO	Carbon Monoxide
CO2	Carbondioxide
CSR	Corperate Social Responsibility
ECPHRFF	European Convention for the Protection of Human Rights and Fundamental Freedoms
EFP	Experimental Fishing Programme
EIA	Environmental Impact Assessment
EITI	Extractive Industries Transparency Initiative
ESIA	Environmental and Social Impact Assessment
ESRB	Electricity Sector Regulatory Board
FDIs	Foreign Direct Investments
GHG	Greenhouse Gas
ICCPR	International Covenant on Civil and Political Rights
ICESCR	International Covenant on Economic, Social and Cultural Rights
ICJ	International Court of Justice
ICMU	Investment Code Management Unit
IOS	International Organisation for Standardisation

LMO	Living Modified Organism
MAGZI	Mission d'Aménagement et de Gestion des Zones Industrielles(Industrial Zones Management Authority)
MINEE	Ministry of Water and Energy Resources
MINMIDT	Ministry of Mines, Industry and Technological Development
MTN	Mobile Telephone Network
N2O	Di nitrogen Oxide
NBSAPV	National Biodiversity Strategy and Action PlanVersion II
NDI	National Democratic Institute for International Affairs
NEMP	National Environmental Management Plan
NOx	Nitrogen
OAU	Organization of African Unity
OECD	Organisation for Economic Cooperation and Development
OHADA	Organisation pour L'Harmonisation en Afrique du Droit des Affaires
ONZFI	l'Office National des Zones Franches Industrielles
PCIJ	Permanent Court of International Justice
PWYP	Publish What You Pay
SBT	Southern Bluefin Tuna
SCDP	SociétéCamerounaise de Dépôts Pétroliers
SNI	Société National d'Investment (National Investîmes Corporation)
SO2	Sulphur Dioxide
ToR	Terms of Reference
UCIL	Union Carbide India Limited
UDHR	Universal Declaration of Human Rights
UN	United Nations
UNESCO	United Nations Educational, Scientific and Cultural Organization
UNFCCC	United Nations Framework Convention on Climate Change
UNGAR	United Nation General Assembly Ressolution
WBCSD	World Business Council for Sustainable Development
WCED	World Commission on Environment and Development
WTO	World Trade Organisation

CHAPTER ONE

GENERAL INTRODUCTION

1.0 Background to Study

The quest for industrialisation in Cameroon has had negative effects on the environment. The effects of different industrial activities on the environment vary enormously but it is an incontrovertible statement that damage is being done to the environment.[1] Cameroon is a country heavily dependent on revenues generated from oil, timber, agricultural products and other natural resources. Ever since the country gained independence, focus has been on sustainable development through industrialisation. In principle the government is bent on alleviating poverty so as to give her citizens the opportunity to live dignified lives. Actions towards this have been directed to creating an enabling environment that permits companies to effectively play their role as catalysts of economic development,[2] and maximisation of revenue generated from its rich resource endowments. This is evident in its desire to establish a favourablelegal environment and demarcate territories for industrial settlement. In line with this objective, the government has engaged herself in myriad policies aimed at attracting foreign capital which is believed to be a booster of economic

[1] Emeka O., Adedoyin, R., and Adeola D. "Environmental Issues and Corporate Social Responsibility. The Nigerian Experience", (2008), *Kamla-Raj Journal of Human Ecology*, 23(2), p. 101-107.

[2] The following structures were set up by the State to provide an institutional framework for the implementation of industrial development strategies: Centre for the Promotion of and Assistance to Small and Medium-sized enterprises (CAPME) set up in 1970, to conduct studies on, and provide assistance to small and medium sized undertakings; The National Investment Corporation, set up in 1964 to manage enterprises in government portfolio, examine public investment projects, orientate the national savings policy and finance investments; The Cameroon Development Bank (CDB) set up in 1961 to finance investment; The National Standardisation Committee set up in 1968 to monitor the implementation and follow-up of standards related issues; The Investment Code Management Unit (ICMU) to monitor the implementation of the Investment Code. Unfortunately, some of these structures such as CAPME and the CDB have disappeared.

development. At national level the government is making efforts to put in place a healthy environment for business.[3] At regional level, with respect to creating a favourable legal environment that would attract and maintain Foreign Direct Investments (FDIs),[4] the government amongst other things, established an Investment Code in 1960[5] and ratified the treaty creating the Organization for the Harmonisation of Business Laws in Africa (better known by its French acronym OHADA)[6] which was created by the Port Louis Treaty.[7] She is a member of the Central African Economic and Monetary Community (better known by its French acronym CEMAC), whose aim[8] is to eliminate barriers to trade so as to boost development in the sub-region.

To provide necessary territorial space to accommodate these companies, the government has carved out industrial free zones.[9] Today Cameroon is host to a large number of multination companies with diverse nationalities[10] and

[3] Law n° 2002/004 of 19th April 2002 instituting the Investment Charter of Cameroon. This law contains incentives to foreign investor who wish to invest in Cameroon.

[4] Most of these come in the form of multinational companies.

[5] The Investment Code of 1960 was instituted by Law No. 60/64 of 27 June 1960. The 1960 Investment Code was first amended in 1964 by Law No. 64/LEF/6 of 6 April 1964 and Law No. 66/LF of 10 June 1966. The second Investment Code was that of 1984 instituted by Law No. 84/003 of 4 July 1984. In 1990, the third Investment Code was instituted by Law No.90/7 of 8 November 1990, ratified into law by Law No. 90/71 of 19 December 1990 as amended. In 1994 there was another Investment Code instituted by Ordinance No. 94/003 of 4 January 1994. The Fourth and current Investment Code applicable in Cameroon is that of 2002. The rationale for this Code known as the Investment Charter is spelt out in the explanatory statement of the Bill to institute the Charter, i.e. Bill No. 714 to institute the Investment Charter. Cameroon has enacted four investment laws since it gained independence in 1960.

[6] Organisation pour L'Harmonisation en Afrique du Droit des Affaires

[7] The Treaty was signed in October 1993 and ratified in 1997.

[8] See Regulation No. 17/99/CEMAC – 020-CM-03 relating to the CEMAC Investment Charter. See precisely the Preamble (The Investment Charter shall be a general framework involving all the measures aimed at ameliorating the institutional, fiscal and financial environment of enterprises so as to promote growth and diversify the economies of member states, on the basis of a better definition of the role of the state and of a harmonious development of the private sector through investments from within and outside the country.)

[9] An industrial zone is a piece of land, geographically demarcated which is developed to receive industries. The handling and treatment of industrial waste is of capital importance in the development of the zone. The Industrial Zones Management Authority (MAGZI) was created by Decree No. 71/DF/95 of March 01, 1971 to acquire, develop and manage industrial zones and putting at the disposal of manufacturers and other economic operators this developed land for the implantation of industrial or commercial enterprises throughout the national territory. MAGZI is presently operating in six regions of Cameroon notably Adamawa, Centre, Littoral, North, West and South West.

[10] By diverse nationality, we are simply referring to the fact that most of these companies especially those that have a large capital base are and multinationals owned by foreigners.

activities[11] with the majority of them located in the Douala metropolitan area.[12]

The effort to attract and maintain these companies to enable them to propel the much needed development has unfortunately not considered the social and environmental consequences of corporate activities. Thus, the intensification of economic activities only increases the danger of environmental degradation to the local communities and consumers at large, which is already evident in several forms. Available literature reveals that the environmental effect resulting from their activities in Cameroon could be seen on all socio-economic sectors, especially in the domains of agriculture, livestock rearing, energy, health, industry, biodiversity[13] and natural resources.[14] Meanwhile, though Cameroon has apparently not yet gain a great degree of environmental consciousness in this light, it is likely to become a major source of water pollution in future.

---

[11] Field of activity here refers to the particular type activity of the industry that may be extractive, manufacturing or service (tertiary).

[12] The Littoral administrative region constitutes the main industrial hub of Cameroon, accounting for 80 percent of industrial plants in the country (with 20 percent spread in the rest of the country).

[13] The contribution of MNCs to biodiversity extinction has been overwhelmingly supported by different scholars whose work reveal that Cameroon faces accelerated loss of biodiversity as the status of its major ecosystems increasingly deteriorate. Statistics show that out of about 9,000 species of plants in Cameroon, some 355 are threatened with extinction; of the estimated 613 species of fish, 112 are threatened with extinction; out of 119 amphibians, 53 are under threat of extinction and of the 968 species of birds 30 face threat of extinction. Republic of Cameroon, "National Biodiversity Strategy and Action Plan Version II MINEPDED" (2012), available at http://www.cbd.int/doc/world/cm/cm- nbsap- v2- en.pdf, (accessed on the 2/10/19).République du Cameroun, "Cinquième Rapport National du Cameroun a la Convention de la Diversité biodiversité, MINEPDED," (2014). Available at http://www.cbd.int/doc/world/cm/cm- nr- 05- fr.pdf(last visited 07/06/2019). The main drivers of biodiversity loss are habitat destruction, agricultural practices, deforestation and forest degradation, desert encroachment, climate change, pollution, unsustainable land use, poaching, erosion and landslides. See generally Eyebe A., Simeon A. E., Angu K. A., and Endamana D., (2012), "Integrating Biodiversity Conservation into National Development Policy: A Case Study of Cameroon," IIED Poverty and Conservation Learning Group Discussion Paper, No. 09.

[14] Norrington-Davies G. "Climate Change Financing and Aid Effectiveness: Cameroon Case Study", (2011), OECD, p. 3, available at www.agulhas.co.uk(last visited 04/05/2019); Molua E. & Lambi C., "The Economic Impact of Climate Change on Agriculture in Cameroon", (2006), *CEEPA Discussion Paper* No. 17, CEEPA, University of Pretoria. See also, Munang T., Rivington M., Bellocchi G., Azam-Ali S., Colls J., "Effects of Climate Change on Crop Production in Cameroon", (2008), *Climate Research*, 36: 65–77; Yong D., "Agriculture and Climate Change in Cameroon: An Assessment of Impacts and Adaptation Options," (2013), p. 85-94.

Meanwhile, though Cameroon has apparently not yet contributed to the current level of global carbon emissions, it is likely to become a major source of pollution in future. Already, average temperatures in Cameroon have been increasing since 1930 with a net increase of 0.95°C between 1930 and 1995.[15] Average rainfall has also decreased by over 2% per decade since 1960.[16] These changes have been blamed on GHG emissions from companies and other sources with the effect being extreme weather conditions across the country.[17]

Statistical data[18] on the rate of emission of Greenhouse Gasses (GHG)[19] into the atmosphere in Cameroon reveals that companies are the third largest emitter of GHG after the energy and agricultural sectors; recording 387.03Gg for Carbon dioxide (CO_2), 0.19Gg for Oxides of nitrogen (NO_x), 11.77Gg for Carbon monoxide (CO) and 1.38 for Sulphur dioxide (SO_2). These figures are said to be on the rise with the growth of the economy and the possibility is that industries would become the highest emitter.[20] Moreover, most companies predominantly sited along water courses and coastal wetlands discharge untreated effluents into these water bodies and as such grossly polluting these medium.[21] As affirmed

[15] Norrington-Davies G. *op. cit.*, p. 3.

[16] *ibid.*

[17] The Northern region is experiencing increasing incidents of drought and desert advancement that have scorched large expanses of land while the Southwest coastal and rainforest regions are experiencing increased periods of prolonged rainfall that have led to flooding. Average annual temperatures are predicted to increase between 1.5°C and 4.5°C by 2100 with a 1.6°C to 3.3°C rise in coastal zones and a 2.1°C to 4.5°C17 rise in the Sahel region.

[18] Youssaou M. (2011). *Les Question Environnementaux sur la Désertification au Cameroun.* Paper presented at the workshop on Statistics of the Environment, Yaoundé, 5-9 December, p. 34.

[19] It should be noted that this study was conducted for five different greenhouse gases, namely, Carbon dioxide (CO2), Methane (CH4), Di nitrogen oxide (N2O), Carbon monoxide (CO) and Oxides of nitrogen (NOx).

[20] This inventory was done at a time when the country had just a few heavy polluting companies and paid attention to just about 25factories. Today, with the liberalisation of the private sector, the number of companies has increased tremendously so too is the percentage of emission. Even at this, many may argue that the emission rate of Cameroon is minimal and negligible when compared to big industrialised nations. Probably, that is why the Kyoto Protocol to the UNFCCC does not set any standard for Cameroon. A justification of this nature could be very misleading because though Cameroon like many other developing countries contributes a negligible percentage of emissions, the country is more vulnerable to the effects of climate change than the industrialised countries. More so, pollution no matter how small, contributes to the destruction of the ozone layer and public health problems.

[21] For example, the Littoral region which constitutes the main industrial hub of Cameroon, accounts for over 70 percent of industrial plants located along the coast.

by Asangwe,[22] utilisation of petroleum products within the designated industrial zones and illegal locations have made the proper discharge of effluents resulting from production processes and transportation a serious environmental problem.[23] These effluents, passing through city drains and spillways, end up in water bodies with resultant damage to aquatic life, contamination of surface water for human consumption, crops and livestock.[24]

It is staggering to note that the limited or none existence of CSR activities in these areas does not affect the profitability of the companies because most of them have monopoly in the market in Cameroon. Several sector businesses are involved in development initiatives to create employment and generate sources of income. Most large businesses such as ENEO, CamWater, MTN, ORANGE, CAMRAIL, Bollore etc. have taken discretionary measures to improve the living conditions of the local population. Increasingly, the employees, consumers and the local communities are expecting a lot from businesses operating in the country and local areas.

The main objective of this study therefore is to contribute to the understanding of environmental issues in relation to the exploitation of electricity and water in Cameroon in particular. The study has been prompted because of evidence to the effect that natural resource exploitation and environmental development are strongly interconnected. The dominant argument or view is that natural resource exploitation should be done in a way that the immediate community from where the resources are exploited should also benefit. The idea is to

---

[22] Asangwe C., "The Douala Coastal Lagoon Complex, Cameroon: Environmental Issues", (2006), available at https://www.fig.net/resources/publications/figpub/pub36/chapters/chapter_9.pdf (visited on the 23/07/2019).

[23] Most of the effluents referred to here are petroleum product effluents which are generally any processes or unprocessed liquid, viscous and gaseous evacuation of agricultural and industrial constituents that contain petroleum input into the environment. These effluents are discharged during processing, transportation and utilisation as hydraulic fluids, solvents, fertilizers, sludge, etc into the predominantly aquatic terrain. These sources of petroleum effluents contain enormous quantities of contaminants ranging from hydrocarbons to trace metals. Some of these trace metals include zinc, copper, cadmium, lead, mercury, nickel, vanadium, phenol, cyanide, arsenic, etc.

[24] Studies in this area indicate that the discharge of untreated effluents with high pollution loads in excess of their assimilative capacities and destroys their ability to support aquatic life. See Chebo, *op. ci.t*, note 21, p. 7.

show that the respect for environmental concerns and human rights when exploiting natural resources can go a long way to reduce poverty and raise the standard of living and create a healthy environment for development within the community from where the resources are exploited. This is consistent with the government policy of poverty reduction and development and also in consonance with the human right to development.

Understandably, this study examines the environmental aspects of corporate social responsible (CSR) in the Energy and water sectors in Cameroon and how that connects to governmental policy. ENEO and CamWater which are the unique hydro-electrical and water corporations in Cameroon are recognised as an impetus to economic, social, cultural and political advancement. Surprisingly, in this strive to achieve economic development, little or no consideration has been given to environmental effects of their activities even when government's principal responsibility has been to ensure social and environmental safety as well as mitigate any damage. Even when social and environmental problems have arisen, they have been minimised "in the public interest". As a result, corporate environmental policies have not occupied a priority position on the agenda of these corporate and its implementation as such is relatively slow. The outcome of this has been the perpetration ofcorporate conduct that is negligent of safeguards that mitigate environmental degradation even when the state has taken measures through legislations to set social and environmental standards in a bid to regulate corporate conducts that contribute to environmental safety to the local communities. While acknowledging the innovations in these laws, we equally argue that this has taken place within the ambit of weak and insufficiently articulated policy. Sanctions and implementation have not been stringent enough to effectively deter ENEO and CamWater from violating CER as corroborated by the increase in the number of cases on violation of CER. This calls for reforms as well as the enforcement of the sanctions system. Adopting an empirical and in-depth analysis of primary and secondary data,this paper therefore examines and evaluates ENEO and CamWater's CER policies and activities in the local communities where they operate having their equipments installed. In fact, the study explores the problems of the people living in these local communities, the expectations they have towards these corporations.

To achieve this broad objective set out herein above, the study will look specifically at the following issues:

- examine the legal framework for regulating Cameroon's hydroelectricity and water industries;
- critically evaluate the level of implementation of CER policies in the hydroelectricity and water sectors;
- examine the need for a healthy environment;
- assess the compliance and enforcement of CER within the hydro-electrical and water sectors;
- identify and discuss the sanctions for violation of corporate environmental responsibility;
- Proposals for reforms.

1.1 Corporate Social Responsibility: A Conceptual Understanding

There is no universally accepted definition of CSR. CSR is difficult to define in concise and precise terms. Little wonder there is no universally acceptable definition of CSR. The definition of the concept varies and different papers and textbooks define it differently, depending on the time the literature was written and the ideological belief behind it. To set a pathway for this paper and avoid confusion in the process, we have provided an operational definition of corporate social responsibility and limit its scope. An attempt would also be made to explore some of the ways it has over the years been used by international bodies, corporate organisations, and academics.

The incorporation of socio-economic and environmental concerns in business is a long standing issue which emanates from the concept of Corporate Social Responsibility (CSR). The concept of corporate social responsibility focuses on conducts of firms towards interests that are not directly related to their goals and objectives, which most often are profit oriented. It justifies the argument of whether corporations owe a duty to stakeholders other than shareholders. This is in accord with Marquis et al.[25] who, citing David, define CSR as "*firm's consideration of, and response to, issues beyond the narrow economic, technical, and legal requirements of the firm to accomplish social benefits along with traditional economic gains which the firm seeks*". Support to this view is leant by the stakeholder theory postulated by Mackey[26] who points out that being socially responsible and ethical is not inconsistent with profit making. As he succinctly puts it, profit making should be the means to an end of creating value for all stakeholders, including employees, customers, suppliers, investors, and communities where the companies operate. This is in contrast with the conservative views of the shareholder theory postulated by economists like Milton Friedman who sees shareholders as principals who hire directors as agents to manage corporations and the job of the directors is to increase shareholders' wealth through every means possible except in violation of the law. In his words, "*there is one and only one social responsibility of business – to use its resources and engage in activities designed to increase its profits so long as it stays within the rules of the game, which is to say, engages in open and free competition without deception or fraud. ...*"[27]

There are many other definitions of CSR circulating and evolving at the same time, which are explicitly and implicitly involving a range of stakeholders (internal, external active and silent ones), different activities (not only of charitable nature) and aims. Perhaps, another definition that is worth considering in this light is that of Carroll and Buchholtz.[28] They define CSR as "*economic, legal, ethical, and discretionary expectations that society has of organisations at a given point in time*". The concept of CSR means that organisations have moral, ethical, and philanthropic responsibilities in

[25] Marquis, C., Glynn, M. A. and Davis, G. F. "Community Isomorphism and Corporate Social Action", (2007), *Academy of Management Review*, 32, 3, pp. 925-945.

[26] Mackey J, "Rethinking the Social Responsibility of Business", (2005), In Reason (online debate with Milton Friedman and T. J. Rodgers). Available at: http://www.reason.com/news/show/32239.html, (accessed 27 August, 2019).

[27] Friedman M., "The Social Responsibility of Business is to Increase its Profits", (1970), *The New York Times Magazine*, Section 6, p. 30, 126-127.

[28] Carroll A. and Buchholtz A., *Business and Society: Ethics and Stakeholder Management*, (Mason, OH: Thomson South-Western, 2003), p. 36.

addition to their responsibilities to earn a fair return for investors and comply with the law.[29] Carroll and Buchholtz's definition presents a multi-faceted nature of social responsibility. To begin with, the economic responsibilities refer to society's expectation that organisations will produce goods and services that are needed and desired by customers and sell those goods and services at a reasonable price. The second is the legal responsibilities which relate to the expectation that organisations will comply with the laws set down by society to govern competition in the marketplace. Thirdly, ethical responsibilities concern societal expectations that go beyond the law, such as the expectation that organisations will conduct their affairs in a fair and just way. Finally, the discretionary responsibilities of corporations refer to society's expectation that organisations be good citizens. This may involve such things as philanthropic support of programs benefiting a community or the nation.[30]

From an organisational perspective, Holmes and Watts[31] on behalf of World Business Council for Sustainable Development (WBCSD) provide a representative definition as the "*continuing commitment by business to behave ethically and contribute to economic development while improving the quality of life of the workforce and their families as well as the local community and the society at large*". According to Business for Social Responsibility (BSR), CSR is defined as "*achieving commercial success in ways that honour ethical values and respect people, communities and the natural environment*".[32]

[29] A traditional view of the corporation suggests that its primary, if not sole, responsibility is to its owners, or stockholders. However, CSR requires organisations to adopt a broader view of its responsibilities that includes not only stockholders but other constituencies as well, including employees, suppliers, customers, the local community, local, state, and federal governments, environmental groups, and other special interest groups. Collectively, the various groups affected by the actions of an organisation are called "stakeholders."

[30] Carroll A., and Buchholtz A., *Business and Society, op. cit.*, pp. 37-38.

[31] Hulms L. and Watts R. (2000), *Corporate Social Responsibility: Making Good Business Sense*, World Business Council for Sustainable Development, Geneva, p. 3.

[32] Business for Social Responsibility (BSR) is a global non-profit organisation funded by corporations. Its goal is to help member companies achieve commercial success in ways that respect ethical values, people, communities and the environment. BSR member companies have nearly $2 trillion in combined annual revenues and employ more than six million workers around the world. See generally, www.bsr.org (accessed on 12/03/2019).

Another organisation that has contributed in expanding the concept of corporate social responsibility and perhaps the most fitting operational definition in the context of this paper is the European Commission. The European Commission Green Paper on CSR of 2010 defines CSR as "*a concept whereby companies decide voluntarily to contribute to a better society and a cleaner environment*".[33] This definition immediately reveals the split in the debate over CSR, namely whether it includes environmental responsibility or whether it runs parallel with working in the area of corporate environmental management. In this light, Welford[34] suggests that CSR must run in parallel with environmental management if companies are to act in a way that is consistent with sustainable development. Similarly, Elkington,[35] stressing the Triple Bottom Line Concept, is very much in line with this approach where there are essentially 'three pillars' in which sustainable development is built. These proponents seem to be pressing on the impression that environmental responsibility is an independent pillar that runs parallel with CSR. However, other proponents of CSR like Mazurkiewicz see it as the all-encompassing 'umbrella term' that engulfs environmental aspects. In effect, Mazurkiewicz[36] in his attempt to define corporate environmental responsibility refers to it as the environmental aspect of CSR in other words corporate environmental responsibility. This paper aligns with the definition of Mazurkiewicz with the view that environmental responsibility is part of CSR. Whether the two concepts are parallel or one is a subset of the other, what is important is that the environment is considered part of the corporate social responsibility, which is the focus of this study.

---

[33] See the European Commission (2001), Promoting a European Framework for Corporate Social Responsibility, *Green Paper*. Available at http:/europa.eu.int/comm./employment_social/soc-dial/csr/greenpaper_en.pdf (accessed on 14/8/2019).

[34] Welford R. (2000), *Corporate Environmental Responsibility 3: Towards Sustainable Development*, Earthscan, London, cited in Welford, R (2003), p. 3.

[35] Elington J. (1997), *Cannibals with Forks: The Triple Bottom Line of the 21st Century Business*, Capstone/Wiley, London, cited in Welford (2003), p.3.

[36] Mazurkiewicz P "Corporate Environmental Responsibility: Is a common CSR framework possible" (2004), DevComm-SDO, World Bank, p. 2.

CHAPTER TWO

REGULATORY FRAMEWORKS ON ELECTRICITY AND WATER SECTORS IN CAMEROON

2.0 Introduction

There is no gain-saying that the industrial sector in Cameroon makes a considerable amount of social and economic contributions. This sector constitutes a major source of direct and indirect employment to many Cameroonians and is equally a source of revenue for the state. However, oneri not be wrong to say that the contribution of the industrial sector to the socio-economic advancement of Cameroon's economy is not without repercussions. Experience reveals that industrial activities, especially pollution continue to inflict a wide range of complications to safety, health and environmental quality.[37] Industries constitute the main sources of greenhouse gas emission and other forms of pollution, contamination of water sources, opening up of forest cover, to name a few.[38]

In collaboration with international agencies and non-governmental organisations, and in keeping with international law, the government of Cameroon has taken measures to articulate environmental governance through corporate social responsibility.

[37] This is most especially the case of the industrial cities of Douala and Yaoundé where most of the companies are concentrated.

[38] Fongwe, Z. N., Ndifor, F., Lambi C. M., Etame, R. M. E., Kanmogne B. K., Industrial Water Pollution: The case of the Ndogbong Industrial District, Douala, (2000), in Lambi, C. M., "Environmental issues: Problems and Prospects", (2000), Unique Printers, Commercial Avenue, Bamenda, Cameroon, p. 7 – 22.

Acknowledging the role environmental protection plays in sustainable development and considering that protection of the environment can better be done *in situ* ; the international community through multilaterally negotiated instruments have enjoined states to take necessary measures in ensuring that the environment is adequately protected within their respective territorial limits. Working towards this goal, and drawing from the spirit of these international instruments, Cameroon has enacted a series of legislations having a bearing on environmental aspects of corporate social responsibility. The legal and institutional regulatory frameworks on environmental governance in Cameroon is based on the traditional normative or command and control type of legislation. As Hillary R[39] puts it, this type of legislation is typified by the control of discharges to the atmosphere, water and land. Command and control, the author argues, succinctly describes the operation of such environmental legislation because while the legislation sets the environmental standards for a certain process or operation, (the command part), inspection is necessary by enforcement authorities to ensure compliance to the standards (the control part). Indeed, it has fundamental principles towards the effective and efficient management of industrial activities.

Before 1992, the protection of the environment in Cameroon was governed by a combination of texts that were inadequate and ill-adapted.[40] These laws were crafted with the objective to protect and provide security for human health and the environment. However, the provisions of these laws show that environmental protection was handled in a frivolous manner. They portrayed a clear imbalance in the objectives set, especially objectives which concerned the protection of the environment and prevention of industrial pollution. Furthermore, none of them provided for attendant measures that

[39] Hillary, R, (1997), "Environmental Management Standards, what do SMEs think"? In ISO 14001 and Beyond, Sheldon C (ed.), Greenleaf, Sheffield, p. 19-44, cited in Alemagi Dieudonne, *Towards a Comprehensive Strategy for the Effective and Efficient Management of Industrial Pollution along the Atlantic Coast of Cameroon*, (Ph.D Thesis, Brandenburg University of Technology Cottbus 2006), p. 139. (Unpublished)

[40] The following pieces of legislations governed the protection of the environment from industrial activities: Law No. 86/008 of 5 July 1986 on Gas and Water Vapour Pressure Equipment; Law No. 89/027 of 27 December 1989 on Toxic Waste; Decree No.76/372 of 2 September 1976 to regulate Establishments Classified as Dangerous, Unhygienic and Obnoxious.

would make it possible to effectively control industrial pollution using efficient technical facilities. In a bid to obliterate these drawbacks and to meet up with the provisions of Agenda 21 of the 1992 summit in Rio de Janeiro, the government of Cameroon took a significant step to improve the legal and regulatory framework pertaining to corporate social responsibility in environmental governance. Consequently, the environmental aspects of social responsibilities of corporate bodies in environmental governance in Cameroon today, are encapsulated in regulations with both general and sectoral attributions. Suffice to say that these legislations have a considerable number of provisions geared at controlling industrial conduct vis-à-vis environment governance.

This seemingly attractive investment climate is further brightened by the availability of natural resources in abundance. It is within this framework that investors are vying for licenses to explore for and exploit electricity and water in Cameroon. The investment climate encourages investors to invest in the exploitation of natural resources. Among all these natural resources (primary goods), this study focuses its analysis on the hydro-electrical and water sectors because of the important place they occupy in the economy and because its exploitation has far reaching socio-economic consequences for both the government and the citizenry. Before these investors qualify to deposit applications to obtain an oneribesn to explore and exploit electricity and water in Cameroon, they must also be duly qualified to do business in Cameroon. In order to qualify to do business in Cameroon, and by extension, qualify to apply for a license to explore and exploit electricity and water resources in Cameroon, an investor must satisfy Cameroonian company law.

There are four basic contract types in the electricity industry: concessions, licences and oneribesn, declaration and the free regime.[41] Each form can be used to accomplish the same purpose. The differences between the types of contracts are of a conceptual nature, mainly with regard to levels of control granted to the foreign contractor, to the compensation arrangements, and to

[41] Section 11 (1), Electricity Law.

the levels of involvement by energy corporations. Similarly, the Water Law makes provision for the usage of Concession Contracts for the exploitation of water.[42]

With respect to concession contracts, the Law[43] provides that they shall be signed for the purpose of authorizing the electricity operator to explore for hydroelectricity. The Ministry of Water and Natural Resources is the competent authority to grant concession and licences.[44] The contract determines the rights and obligations of the State and the electricity company throughout the duration of the contract. Any interesting party who intends to conduct an activity intended for the generation of hydroelectric power in particular on public land, the applicant needs to hold a right to exploit it. Consequently, its condition of suspension, duration, expiry, revision, renewable and cancellation as well as the settlement of disputes is determined by the granting authority.[45] The electricity operator finances all the oneribesn operations and disposes of the energy extracted during the validity of the contract, in conformity with the terms of the concession contract, taking into account the right of the State to receive royalties.[46] By virtue of Section 14 (1) of the Electricity Law, owners of hydroelectricity power plants are eligible when retaned through a call for tenders in conformity with regulation in force.

When an electricity or water company has successfully signed either a Concession contract, it can then start its activity in either exploring or exploiting the resources. At this stage, the company is governed both by domestic laws as well as some rules of international law applicable to the electricity and water corporations. They also operate subject to the contract provisions.

Whether these initiatives are completely successful is still a matter of debate. Our preoccupation here is to ascertain : (i) what legal initiatives have been adopted by the government of Cameroon to make companies environmentally

[42] Article 2 (3), Water Law.
[43] *Ibid.*
[44] Section 11 (3), Electricity Law.
[45] Section 13 (2), Electricity Law.
[46] Section 11 (2), Electricity Law.

responsible ? (ii) Are there any sectoral conflicts between the different governmental regulations ? (iii) Are the provisions of the law sufficiently clear and concise in its effort at handling the issue under consideration ?. This can only be answered by examining the legal and institutional frameworks in place.

2.1 LOCAL LEGISLATIONS

2.1.1 Cameroon's Constitution

Since independence and the reunification of former southern Cameroons and French Cameroon in 1972, the country witnessed at least three different constitutions, which are the 1960, 1961, 1972 and the 1996 Constitutions and numerous constitutional amendments. The Constitution of the Republic of Cameroon[47] does not explicitly provide for the right to electricity and water. The constitution of Cameroon is one of those instruments with general attribution that attaches a lot of importance to environmental protection. Before 1996, the protection of the environment and the protection and promotion of the third generation of universal rights to a healthy environment had never been a constitutional concern. They are now enshrined in the preamble of the Constitution of 1996[48]. The Cameroonian Constitution of 1996 provides in the preamble that :

> Every person shall have a right to a healthy environment. The protection of the environment shall be the duty of every citizen. The state shall ensure the protection and improvement of the environment.[49]

---

[47] Law No. 2008/001 of 14 April 2008 to amend and supplement some provisions of Law No. 97/6 of 18 January 1996 to amend the Constitution of 2 June 1972.

[48] Law No. 96/06 of 18 January 1996 to amend the 1992 Constitution of the Republic of Cameroon. Professor Maurice KAMTO has argued with vehemence that the 1996 Constitution is a new written constitution and not a revision of the 1972 Constitution. See his article entitled "Revision Constitutionnelle en Ecriture d'une Nouvelle Constitution", Lex-lata, No. 023-024 du Fevrier/Mars 1996, p. 17-20.

[49] Paragraph 20 of the Preamble of the 1996 Constitution of Cameroon.

As an integral part of environmental law, the right to electricity and water have a comfortable foundation in the constitutional provisions. This could be justified, therefore by the fact that, the constitution makes implicit reference to the right to electricity or water by explicitly making reference to a right to a healthy environment as well as the protection of the environment shall be the duty of every citizen. "Citizen" can refer to: (1) those under colonial occupation, (2) a portion of the population, especially indigenous peoples, (3) the whole of the population, or (4) a synonym for the state.[50] While each of these interpretations has merit and clearly applies in certain contexts, this study asserts that in relation to principle of permanent sovereignty over natural resources , "peoples" is used to encompass a country's whole population who therefore are the rightful owners of her electricity and water, entitled to the benefits accruing there from.

That states shall ensure the protection and improvement of the environment.[51] Therefore, in this light, there is an implicit commitment to protect and improve on the right to electricity and water.

The principle of permanent sovereignty over natural resources as a right has been viewed alternatively as a right vested exclusively in peoples, solely in states (or nations), or jointly in peoples and states. Does the right to electricity and water belong to Cameroonians, to the State or jointly to Cameroonians and the State? By dint of this reasoning therefore, Cameroonians and the state are holders of this right.

This joint vestiture seems to be justified on the basis of the interplay of internal and external factors in matters of economic self-Determination.[52] The state acts as an intermediary in dealings with external interests on behalf of the people in a way that is essentially impossible for the people to do themselves.

---

[50] *Ibid.* See also James A. Graff, Human Rights, Peoples, and the Right to Self-Determination, in Group Rights 186, 186 (Judith Baker ed., 1994).

[51] *Supra.*

[52] Kiwanuka, *supra*, at 95

Cameroon's national legislation[53] arrogates the right to natural resources generally to the State. However, this right is a right of sovereignty rather than a right of ownership stricto senso.

This is in consonance with international law as evidenced by the oneribe of norms provided for by Article 45 of the 1996 Constitution of Cameroon. The concept of ownership entails the right to enjoy, manage and dispose of property in a manner deemed necessary.

2.1.2 The Electricity Law

The main piece of legislation governing the electricity industry and particularly the hydroelectricity in Cameroon is Law No. 2011/022 of 14 December 2011,[54] governing the electricity sector in Cameroon. The Law in its Part I, lays down general activities attached to electricity sector.[55] It provides that the holder of a concession contract to operate a hydroelectricity plant, must conduct its activities with due diligence, taking into considerations the rules of international law and practice applicable to the industry. With respect to concession contracts, the Law[56] provides that they shall be signed for the purpose of oneribes the electricity operator to explore for hydroelectricity. The Ministry of Water and Natural Resources is the competent authority to grant concession and licences.[57] The contract determines the rights and obligations of the State and the electricity company throughout the duration of the contract. Any interesting party who intends to conduct an activity intended for the generation of hydroelectric power in particular on public land, the applicant needs to hold a right to exploit it. Consequently, its condition of suspension, duration, expiry, revision, renewable and cancellation as well as the settlement of disputes is determined by the granting authority.[58] The

[53] See generally the preamble of the 1996 Constitution. See also Art, 3 of Law No. 99/013, instituting the Petroleum Code of Cameroon.

[54] Herein referred to as Electricity Law.

[55] See Michel Nyoth Hiol, 'Le Droit Camerounais de l'Energie', In Environmental Law and Policy in Cameroon –Towards making –Towards making Africa the Tree of Life, (Oliver C. Ruppel Emmanuel D. Kam Yogo [eds./dir.) Germany, Nomos Verlagsgesellschaft, 2018.

[56] *Ibid.*

[57] Section 11 (3), Electricity Law.

[58] Section 13 (2), Electricity Law.

electricity operator finances all the oneribesn operations and disposes of the energy extracted during the validity of the contract, in conformity with the terms of the concession contract, taking into account the right of the State to receive royalties.[59] By virtue of Section 14 (1) of the Electricity Law, owners of hydroelectricity power plants are eligible when retained through a call for tenders in conformity with regulation in force.

With respect to environmental issues, the Law obliges the holder of a concession contract in all circumstances to conduct its activities in such a way as to conserve natural resources and the essential characteristics of the environment and consumerprotection.[60] Since operations associated with the exploration and exploitation of oil has a potential to damage the environment, the contract holder is obliged to undertake an environmental impact assessment prior to the commencement of activities.[61] This study permits the electricity company to evaluate the direct and indirect consequences of the hydroelectricity activities on the ecological equilibrium and on the social life of local inhabitants. Companies definitely go beyond the legal obligation so as to reassure the local communities that hydroelectricity exploitation will benefit them.

2.1.3 Water Law

The Cameroonian legislator passed the Water Law[62] within the respect of environmental and management principles and public health protection. According to the statute, water is a property of the common heritage of the nation[63] for which the state should ensure the protection and management and facilitate access for all. The measures of protection are clearly spelled out in the statute[64] ; and violators come under heavy criminal sanctions[65] with prejudice to civil claims. Cameroon Water Law of April 1998 insists

[59] Section 11 (2), Electricity Law.
[60] Section 1 (2) (d), Electricity Law.
[61] Article 83, Water Law.
[62] Law No. 98/005 of 14 April 1998. Law N° 98/005 of 14 April1998 to lay down the Water Code and its Enabling Statutes.
[63] Article 2 (1), Water Law.
[64] Articles 4-7, Water Law.
[65] Articles 19-20, Water Law.

on the protection, preservation of water sources and the provision of good drinking water to the population.[66] The Water Law expressly contemplates the state's ability to transfer its obligations to manage water resources to local authorities and other entities.[67] To ensure conservation, protection and sustainable utilisation, the code institutes a National Water Committee,[68] an institution placed under the Ministry in charge of Water Resources.
Further, the law distinguishes the different types of water that it governs. They are ;

- Surface water shall mean run-off water ;
- Groundwater shall mean infiltration water;
- Spring water shall mean water sold for human consumption, containing traces of minerals or not, with or without soda, irrespective of their therapeutic properties;
- Mineral water shall mean ground water containing dissolved minerals with therapeutic properties.[69]

It also examines the various causes and substances which may cause water pollution and demands that measures be taken to prevent water pollution. Article 6(1) states that any natural or legal person, owner of facilities likely to cause water pollution, must take all necessary measures to limit or remove the effects. The quality of water is another common feature of the Water Law. It provides that the quality of drinking water is controlled, at all moment, by the administrative body responsible for water and public health.[70]

The government passed several water resource-related decrees in 2001 ; Decree No.2001/161/PM 8 May 2001 which established the powers, organisation and functioning of the National Water Committee ; Decree No. 2001/162/PM 8 My 2001 which sets rules protecting areas around abstracting points and standards for processing and storage of water ; Decree

[66] *Ibid.*
[67] Article 2 (2), Water Law.
[68] Article 26 (1), Water Law.
[69] Article 3, Water Law.
[70] Article 12, Water Law.

No. 2001/162/PM 8 May 2001 specifying terms and conditions of water extraction, surface or groundwater for industrial and commercial uses ; and Decree No. 2001/162/PM 8 May 2001 which specifies rules for the protection of surface or groundwater against pollution.

2.1.4 The Environmental Law

Another piece of legislation with general attribution which articulates environmental governance through corporate social responsibility is the framework law on environmental management in Cameroon.[71] This law which came into force several months after the revised constitution of January 1996 can be said to have been inspired by the constitutional provisions encouraging and strengthening environmental protection. Law No. 96/12 of August 1996 now provides the legal framework for environmental management in Cameroon. This is the first comprehensive law on environmental management in Cameroon and it addresses diverse aspects of the environment. It is interesting to note that this legislation has a considerable number of provisions geared at controlling industrial pollution.

This law incorporates some fundamental international environmental principles which include the Precautionary Principle,[72] the Preventive Action and Precautionary Principle,[73] the Polluter Pay Principle[74] and the Participatory Principle[75] which serve as foundation for the introduction of preventive, precautionary and curative responsibilities on companies. They all play a vital role in combating industrial degradation of the environment in Cameroon. The law in paragraph 3 of Section 9 (e) stipulates that "*corporate bodies and private citizens shall, in all their activities conform to the same requirements*". This provision ascertains the determination of the state through the legislator to respect environmental provisions.

[71] Law No. 96/12 of 5th August 1996 Relating to Environmental Management in Cameroon and Decrees of implementation and Decree No 2005/0577/PM of 23 February 2005, fixing the Modalities for the Realisation of Environmental Impact Assessment.
[72] Part I, Chapter III, Article 9 (a), Environmental Law.
[73] Section 9 (b), Part I, Chapter III, Environmental Law
[74] See Section 9 (c), Part I, Chapter III, Environmental Law.
[75] Section 9 (e), Environmental Law.

Apart from confiding on the state the responsibility to prepare environmental policies and coordinate their implementation, this law equally enjoins the state with the task of drawing up a National Environmental Management Plan (NEMP) which defines policies, objectives and strategies for a more sustainable development in Cameroon. The law further articulates environmental responsibilities in corporate social responsibilities, ranging from preventive to curative responsibilities for corporate bodies.

To begin with, the Environmental Law dedicates a whole chapter to Environmental Impact Assessment (EIA). Section 17 provides *inter alia* that :

> The promoter or owner of any development, labour, equipment or project which may endanger the environment owing to its dimension, nature or the impact of its activities on the natural environment shall carry out an impact assessment, pursuant to the prescriptions of the specifications. This assessment shall determine the direct or indirect incidence of the said project on theecological balance of the zone where the plant is located…[76]

Environmental impact assessment is a procedure that seeks to ensure the acquisition of adequate and early information on the likely environmental consequences of development projects, on possible alternatives, and on measures to mitigate harm.[77] It is mandatory on the promoter to carry out impact assessment. This section of the law does not expressly use the word company or corporate body but does not exclude them either, since most projects in the areas identified by the law are usually executed by corporate bodies because they obviously have the financial might and the technological knowhow to do so. Also, Section 18 is to the effect that impact assessment that does not comply with the prescriptions of the specifications shall be null and void. The law elaborates the content of impact assessment but delegates to a

---

[76] Section 17(1), Environmental Law.

[77] Christopher F. Tamasang & Sylvain N. Atanga, 'Environmental Impact Assessment under Cameroonian Law', In Environmental Law and Policy in Cameroon – Towards Making Africa the Tree of Life, (Oliver C. Ruppel Emmanuel D. Kam Yogo [eds./dir.) Germany, Nomos Verlagsgesellschaft, 2018.

subsequent Ministerial Decree (Decree of implementation)[78] the duty to set detailed procedure for conducting impact assessment and for determining the types of projects that must be submitted to total or partial impact assessment.[79]

Furthermore, by way of preventing environmental destruction and encouraging corporate environmental governance through environmental responsibility in corporate social responsibility, the law provides that :

> In order to avoid atmospheric pollution, buildings, agricultural, industrial, commercial and cottage industrial establishments, vehicles, or other movable objects possessed, exploited or owned by any private individual or corporate body will be constructed, exploited or used in a way as to meet the technical norms in force or established in application of this law or special instruments.[80]

The reading of these sections give a clear understanding and interpretation that environmental standards and minimum required conduct have been set for the construction, exploitation and use of buildings, agricultural, industrial commercial and cottage industrial establishments whether owned by physical persons or corporate bodies with the objective of curtailing atmospheric pollution and protecting the environment.

Part III Section II of the 1996 Law is dedicated to the protection of continental waters and flood plains. Of key importance here, are the provisions of Section 30 sub section 3, paragraphs 1, 2, and 3. Section 30 provides that an enabling decree[81] of this law shall draw up the list of harmful or dangerous substances produced in Cameroon whose direct or indirect discharge, spilling, dumping, immersion or introduction into Cameroonian continental waters are either

---

[78] Decree No. 2005/0577/PM of 23 February 2005, Fixing the Modalities for the Realisation of Environmental Impact Assessment.

[79] See generally, Section 19 (2) of the Environmental Code. See also Section 19 (1).

[80] Section 22 (1), Environmental Code.See also Section 22 (2) & (3), Environmental Code.

[81] This Decreeis Décret No. 2011/2585/PM du 23 Aout 2011, Fixant des Liste des Substances Nocives ou Dangereuses et le Régime de leur Rejet dans les eaux Continentales. This Decree has outlined a list of harmful or dangerous substances produced in Cameroon whose direct or indirect discharge, spilling, dumping, immersion or introduction into Cameroonian continental waters are either prohibited or subject to prior authorisation.

prohibited or subject to prior authorisation.[82] Sub section 3 (1) of Article 30, while referring expressly to industrial plants stipulates that : "*Plants discharging waste waters into Cameroonian continental waters established before the promulgation of this law shall conform to the regulations within a time limit laid down by an enabling decree of this law*".[83]

Apart from the duty imposed by the law on corporate bodies or project executors to effectively conduct environmental impact assessment before execution, companies are expected to establish environmental management plans that will help them to monitor their environmental activities. Generally, however, the duty to monitor environment activities and compliance is vested on the government of Cameroon.[84] Further, in compliance with the provisions of Section 7[85], corporate institutions are also charged with the duty to report their environmental activities. This is equally guaranteed by the fact that it is required of the results of every environmental impact assessment report to be made public after approval by the inter-ministerial committee. In support of this, Section 43 (2) states that :

> Besides, the person shall inform the public of the effects of waste production, owning, elimination or recycling on the environment and public health, pending the rules of confidentiality and the measures intended to prevent or compensate its negative effects.[86]

Another area that the law obliges corporate bodies in a bid to check their activities vis a vis the environment is in the area of wastes management. To this effect, the law provides that waste management will, henceforth, be carried out according to precise technical prescriptions and under the supervision of the Administration. These wastes will, at all times, "be treated in an ecologically rational manner in order to eliminate or mitigate

---

[82] Section 30 (1), Environmental Code.
[83] See generally, Section 30 (1), (2) & (3), Environmental Law.
[84] *Ibid*, Section 10 (2), Environmental Law,
[85] This section provides that "*All persons shall have the right to be informed on the negative effects of harmful activities on man, health, and the environment as well as on the measures taken to prevent or compensate for these effects*".
[86] See generally, Section 43, Environmental Law.

their harmful effect on the health of the population, the natural resources, the fauna and flora and on the quality of the environment in general.[87] Another important area which the Environmental Law has not been silent about is resonant and olfactory nuisances, which have either been banned or are being controlled by specific regulatory instruments.[88] The provisions of the Environmental Law are geared towards establishing an ecologically sustainable industrial development in Cameroon. In trying to push further the importance of protecting the environment, the legislator, through the Environmental Code equally makes provisions for economic and fiscal incentives as a fundamental strategy to reducing pollution emanating from industries in Cameroon.

Moves to realise the implementation of this law have been made through the establishment of certain laws and decrees. Amongst these regulations are : Law No. 98/015 of 14 July 1998 on Establishments Classified as Dangerous, Unhygienic and Obnoxious and it's enabling decree which calls for a study on the dangerous nature of the establishment as well as its impact on the environment ; Decree No. 2005/0577/PM of 23 February 2005 Fixing the Modalities for the Realisation of Environmental Impact Assessment ; Order No. 0069/MINEP of March 2005 by the Minister of Environment and Nature Protection prescribing the different categories of projects that would necessitate an EIA to name a few. Beside these are equally many sectoral laws aimed at achieving the same goal.

2.2 Rules of International Law

In addition to domestic legislation regulating expressly or implicitly the electricity and water industries, there also exist rules of international law, which regulate the activities of these companies operating in Cameroon. These rules for the purpose of convenience can be examined under 'hard law' and 'soft law'.

---

[87] Section 42, Environmetal Law.
[88] See Section 60 and 61, Environmental Law

2.2.1 Soft Law

Soft laws are rules of international law which are not legally binding, but which are respected as a matter of custom. These rules emanate from international organisations such as the United Nations (UN), The Organisation for Economic Cooperation and Development (OECD), and the World Trade Organisation (WTO).

With respect to the OECD, the Guidelines for Multinational Enterprises (the Guidelines) are recommendations addressed by governments to multinational enterprises. They provide voluntary principles and standards for responsible business conduct consistent with applicable laws. The Guidelines aim to ensure that the operations of these enterprises are in harmony with government policies, to strengthen the basis of mutual confidence between enterprises and the societies in which they operate, to help improve the foreign investment climate and to enhance the contribution to sustainable development made by multinational enterprises. The Guidelines are part of the OECD Declaration on International Investment and Multinational Enterprises the other elements of which relate to national treatment, conflicting requirements on enterprises, and international investment incentives and disincentives.

However, the Organisation for Economic Cooperation and Development Guidelines for Multinational Enterprises which are regarded as the only existing code of conduct for international business are, as the name suggests, guidelines only and are not legally binding on MNCs. They are voluntary in nature. The voluntary and non binding nature of the Guidelines has led to criticisms that they do not represent a genuine attempt to control MNCs but are rather designed to deflect criticisms of their activities.[89] A further criticism is that the very objective of the OECD is to protect business and this, according to some observers, is made clear in the Guidelines.[90] The initiation of a Multilateral Agreement on Investment (MAI) within the OECD

[89] R. Jenkins, 'Corporate Code of conduct: self-regulation in a Global Economy', UNRISD Programme on Technology, Business and Society. Paper No. 2. April 2001, p. 4.

[90] E. V. K. Fitzgerald, 'Regulating Large International Firms' UNRISD Programme on Technology, Business and society, Paper No. 5, November 2001, p. 13.

in 1995 appeared to give much credence to the criticism that the objective of the OECD is to protect business and the Guidelines merely designed to deflect criticisms.

2.2.1.1 The United Nations Organisation

Another international oneribesn that is worth examining is the United Nations Organisation (UN). This is the world's most representative body with a potential to control MNCs. The UN attempted to control MNCs through the use of codes of conduct, but this approach was abandoned with the abolition of the United Nations Commission on Transnational Corporations in 1994. Unfortunately, the UN changed its policy from regulation of MNCs to facilitation of foreign direct investment and eventually to co-operation with business following the establishment of the Global Compact by the UN secretary general in 1999. Thus, the UN prefers co-regulation and self-regulation by business over the use of legally binding frameworks. For example, like the Global Compact, the UN Norms on the Responsibilities of Transnational Corporations and Other Business Enterprises with Regard to Human Rights, adopted by the UN Sub-Commission for the Protection and Promotion of Human Rights in 2003, are not legally binding.[91]

The UN General Assembly Resolution 3281 provides in article 2 (2) (b) that each State has the right to regulate and supervise the activities of transnational corporations within its national jurisdiction and take measures to ensure that such activities comply with its laws, rules and regulations and conform with its economic and social policies. It goes further to provide that transnational corporations shall not intervene in the internal affairs of the host State.[92] On its part, UN General Assembly Resolution 1803 provides in part that where authorization to invest is granted to foreign capital, such capital and the earnings on such capital shall be governed by the terms thereof (terms

---

[91] Edwin Mujih, The Regulation of Multinational Corporations operating in Developing Countries: A Case Study of the Chad-Cameroon Pipeline Project, Social Responsibility: An International Journal, 2004

[92] GA Res.3281 (xxix), 29th Sess., Supp. No.31 (1974)

of the oneribesn), by national legislation in force and by international law. It further provides that the profit derived must be shared in the proportion freely agreed upon, in each case, between the investor and the recipient State, due care being taken to ensure that there is no impairment, for any reason, of that State's sovereignty over its natural wealth and resources.[93] Equally Resolution 3202 makes provision for the regulation and control of the activities of transnational corporations.[94] However, a controversy surrounds the binding nature of these GA resolutions. The UN Charter does not contain any general provisions on the legal effects of GA resolutions. Opinion is therefore divided over the issue as to whether UNGA resolutions are binding or not. Proponents of the non-binding nature of UNGA resolutions[95] have argued that:

> All that the GA resolution can do is to discuss and recommend and initiate studies and consider reports from other bodies. It cannot act on behalf of all the members as the Security Council does and its decisions are not directions, telling the member states what they are, or are not to do. In principle, its functions are similar to those of the assembly of the League and like that body, must rely on cooperation among members and not on power for it has no power.[96]

2.2.1.2 World Trade Organisation

The World Trade Organiation (WTO) is another oneribesn that seeks to protect rather than regulate MNCs. As the most important body involved in international regulation of commerce, the WTO seems to be the only international body with real power to enforce judgments against MNCs, thus effectively regulating them. Unfortunately, the devotion of the WTO to free trade means that it is seen by some critics as part of the problem rather than

[93] Article 1 (3) of General Assembly Resolution 1803 (XVII) of 14 December 1962, on Permanent Sovereignty over Natural Resources.
[94] See Part V of UN General Assembly Resolution 3202 on the Programme of Action on the Establishment of a New International Economic Order, May 1 1974
[95] J. L. Briely and D.H.N Johnson
[96] J.L. Briely, The Law of Nations, …

the solution, as most of its decisions have been in favour of MNCs.[97] The WTO agreements cover goods, services and intellectual property. They spell out the principles of liberalisation, and the permitted exceptions. They include individual countries' commitments to lower customs tariffs and other trade barriers, and to open and keep open services markets. They set procedures for settling disputes. They prescribe special treatment for developing countries. They require governments to make their trade policies transparent by notifying the WTO about laws in force and measures adopted, and through regular reports by the secretariat on countries' trade policies. These agreements are often called the WTO's trade rules, and the WTO is often described as "rules-based", a system based on rules. But it is important to remember that the rules are actually agreements that governments negotiated.

The rules and resolutions emanating from these organisations are not binding, although there is controversy as to the binding nature of United Nations General Assembly Resolutions.

2.2.2 Hard Law

Hard law here refers to binding rules of international law as may be found in instruments like the United Nations Charter, the Universal Declaration of Human Rights, the International Covenant on Civil and Political Rights, the International Covenant on Economic, Social and Cultural Rights, and the African Charter on Human and Peoples' Rights. Cameroon has signed and ratified all these instruments.

Although the existence of the norms embodied in these documents cannot be denied, there has been controversy about their binding character and practical effect. L. B. Sohn argues[98] in particular, that most of these documents are 'soft law,' rather than 'hard law.' According to this view, these documents contain no more than mere guidelines, which states need not follow. Furthermore, there are no effective means of implementing the

---

[97] *Ibid.* at 95

[98] Louis B. Sohn, The New International Law: Protection of the Rights of Individuals rather than States, 32 Am. U. L. Rev. 1,1982

documents, and violators go unpunished.[99] The better view definitely is that these documents have become a part of international customary law and, as such, are binding on all states. Some of the documents provide appropriate means of implementation, leading to a proper condemnation of violators. It is difficult to proceed against great sovereign states, and even more difficult to punish them in any meaningful fashion. States function through individuals, however, and eventually means are likely to be found to punish those who are truly responsible for a state's misbehavior. Although law ideally treats all parties equally, it is well known that the legal enforcement system is less effective against those who are powerful than against those who are poor and weak. Victor Hugo described this in his great romances, *The Count of Monte Cristo and Les Miserables*.[100] Emile Zola and Charles Dickens observed that even domestic law is imperfect in this respect.[101] It is also well known that powerful multinational corporations and great transnational consortia often have been able to act outside the law, with only minor punishments. Once governments became willing to enforce stronger sanctions, punishing responsible officers as well as the corporations themselves led to more cautious attitudes on the part of officers.

On the international scene, it is difficult to persuade governments, which as a group are the international lawmakers, to agree on enforcement against themselves in the event that they violate international law. It is not the law that is soft, but the governments are soft. Usually hiding behind the vital interests of the state, 'raison d'état,' they find it difficult to declare punishable an act that they may someday wish to commit.

---

[99] *Ibid.*

[100] *Ibid.*

[101] See, C. DICKENS, BLEAK HOUSE (1853). The following passage demonstrates Dickens' dim view of the legal system: This is the Court of Chancery; which has its decaying houses and its blighted lands in every shire; which has its worn-out lunatic in every madhouse, and its dead in every churchyard; which has its ruined suitor, with his slipshod heels and threadbare dress, borrowing and begging through the round of every man's acquaintance; which gives to monied might the means abundantly of wearying out the right; which so exhausts finances, patience, courage, hope; so overthrows the brain and breaks the heart; that there is not an honourable man among its practitioners who would not give—who does not often give—the warning, 'Suffer any wrong that can be done you, rather than come here!'Id. at 6-7. See also E. ZOLA, GERMINALE (1885).

2.2.2.1 The United Nations Charter

Although it is easy to wave off the Charter of the United Nations with the back of the hand and stigmatize it as being ineffective, most critics seem not to have reviewed the Charter carefully enough and, therefore, do not have a mastery of its exact content. This constitution of the world, the highest instrument in the intertwined hierarchy of international and domestic documents, prevails expressly over all other treaties, and implicitly over all laws, anywhere in the world.[102] The Charter was not meant to be a temporary document, to be easily and perpetually amended, but, rather, to be a lasting expression of the needs of humanity as a whole. Its basic provisions, constituting the *jus cogens*, are broad in scope and sufficiently flexible to permit their interpretation to be adjusted to the needs of each generation. It is no secret that although the wording of the Charter has changed little since its inception, only with respect to the membership of its two executive organs, the meanings of several provisions have been greatly expanded in practice by commonly accepted interpretations. In attempting to explain this scenario, L. B. Sohn contends that:

> As nature abhors a vacuum, constitutional documents abhor strait-jackets. Great ideas cannot be imprisoned; they must be able to move freely from one part of the earth to another. The U.N. Charter contains several such ideas, which revolutionized the world, although no one knew in 1945 how successful the drafters of the Charter would be in planting in that document the seeds from which many mighty trees would grow.[103]

The most influential of these ideas are that human rights are of international concern, and that the United Nations has the duty to promote 'universal respect for, and observance of, human rights and fundamental freedoms for all without distinction as to race, sex, language and religion.'[104] It is the duty of the international community not only to respect human rights but also to promote their 'universal respect' and to ensure that they are

[102] U.N. Charter, Article 103.
[103] Cf. note 44, supra, at 6
[104] U.N. Charter, art.55(c).

observed throughout the globe.[105] All members of the United Nations—not only the original 50, but the more than 150 members today—have pledged to 'take joint and separate action,' in cooperation with the United Nations for the achievement of these great purposes.[106] In the Charter's preamble, the peoples of the United Nations as well as their governments have reaffirmed their 'faith in fundamental human rights, in the dignity and worth of the human person, in the equal rights of men and women and of nations large and small.'[107] In that statement the authors of the Charter anticipated not only the racial revolution, but also the dignity and worth of the human person. The charter therefore anticipated that the human person had the right to lead a dignified life as well as live in an environment free from contamination. It implies that all peoples, both physical and moral, have to take measures to ensure that this should be the case. The United Nations deals principally with nation states. However, the various nation states are made up of different constituent parts. Hence, the aspirations of the United Nations Charter are to be applicable on these various constituent parts.

2.2.2.2 The Universal Declaration of Human Rights

Although the U.N. Charter mentions human rights in many places, it did not prepare a more detailed document paralleling the national bills or declarations of the rights of man and of the citizen. It was promised at San Francisco that the United Nations would commence the drafting of an International Bill of Rights as one of the first items of business. The Commission on Human Rights was established in 1946, only a few months after the Charter came into force, and was asked to prepare such a document.[108] It soon became obvious that the task could take a long time and, in view of the urgency of the matter, that the first step should be a declaration of general principles, to be followed later by a document containing more precise obligations.

---

[105] *Ibid.*
[106] *Ibid.* Article 56.
[107] *Ibid.* preamble.
[108] E.S.C. Res. 5(I), 1 U.N. ESCOR Supp. (No. 1) at 163, U.N. Doc. E/1 (1946).

Two years later the first document, the Universal Declaration of Human Rights,[109] was ready. On December 10, 1948, the General Assembly, after some amendments, approved it unanimously. Although some delegations emphasized that the Universal Declaration of Human Rights was not a treaty imposing legal obligations,[110] others more boldly argued that it was more than an ordinary General Assembly resolution, that it was a continuation of the Charter and shared the dignity of that basic document. It merely expressed more forcefully rules that already were recognized by customary international law. Under the latter view, the Declaration would possess a binding character.[111] In particular, Professor Cassin, one of the principal authors of the Declaration, explained that the Declaration was 'destined to guide Governments in the determination of their policy and their national legislation,' that it 'could be considered as an authoritative interpretation of the Charter of the United Nations and as the common standard to which the legislation of all the Member States of the United Nations should aspire,' and that it 'was a development of the Charter which had brought human rights within the scope of positive international law.'[112] The Declaration itself proclaims that it is 'a common standard of achievement for all peoples and all nations.' It calls upon every individual and every organ of society to strive, 'by progressive measures, national and international, to secure . . . universal and effective recognition and observance of the rights and freedoms therein'.[113]

Even if governments and scholars were originally in disagreement regarding the importance, status, and effect of the Universal Declaration, practice in the United Nations soon caught up with the doubters. Several of the governments

[109] Approved December 10, 1948, G.A. Res. 217A, U.N. Doc.A/810 at 56 (1948) [hereinafter cited as Universal Declaration]. Among the rights included in the Universal Declaration are the following: the right to life, liberty, and security of person (art. 3); the right to be free from arbitrary arrest, detention, or exile (Article 9); the right to marry and found a family (art. 16); the right to freedom of thought, conscience, and religion (Article 18); and the right to education (Article 26).

[110] Mrs. Roosevelt was obliged to state on behalf of the United States that the Declaration 'was not a treaty or international agreement and did not impose legal obligations.' 3 U.N. GAOR (pt. 1, 3d Comm.) at 22 (1948).

[111] Louis B. Sohn, AShort History of the United Nations Documents on Human Rights, in COMMISSION TO STUDY THE ORGANIZATION OF PEACE, 18TH REPORT, THE UNITED NATIONS AND HUMAN RIGHTS 39, 68-70 (1968).

[112] *Ibid* at 70

[113] Universal Declaration, *supra.*

that originally were skeptical about the value of the Declaration did not hesitate to invoke it against other countries. Thus, the United States invoked it in the so-called *Russian Wives Case*, and the General Assembly declared that Soviet measures preventing Russian wives from leaving the Soviet Union in order to join their foreign husbands were 'not in conformity with the Charter,' citing articles 13 and 16 of the Declaration in support of its conclusion.[114] The Soviet Union, which originally claimed that the Declaration violated the Charter's prohibition against interference in a state's internal affairs, later voted for many resolutions charging South Africa with violations of the Universal Declaration.[115]

The Declaration thus is now considered to be an authoritative interpretation of the U.N. Charter, spelling out in considerable detail the meaning of the phrase 'human rights and fundamental freedoms,' which Member States agreed in the Charter to promote and observe. The Universal Declaration has joined the Charter of the United Nations as part of the constitutional structure of the world community. The Declaration, as an authoritative listing of human rights, has become a basic component of international customary law, binding on all states, not only on members of the United Nations. Thus, multinationals, and by extension oil multinationals operating across borders are answerable to this international constitution.

2.2.2.3 The African Charter on Human and Peoples' Rights

The African Charter on Human and Peoples' Rights, also known as the Banjul Charter on Human and Peoples' Rights, was adopted by the 18th Assembly of Heads of State and Government of the Organization of African Unity (OAU), held in Nairobi in June 1981. It entered into force on October 21, 1986, after the deposit of the 26th instrument of ratification, the number required by its Article 63(3). By April 16, 1987, there were 33 states parties to the Charter,[116]

[114]. G.A. Res. 285(III), U.N. Doc. A/900 (1949).
[115] See, S.C. Res. 182, 18 U.N. SCOR Supp. (Oct.-Dec. 1963) at 103, U.N. Doc. S/5471 (1963).
[116] See Richard N. Kiwanuka, The Meaning of 'People' in the African Charter of Human and Peoples' Rights, 82 Am. J. Int'l L., 1988, at 1

which makes it the largest regional human rights system in existence.[117] This is a regional instrument which is binding on member States of the African Union. It provides in its article 21 that:

1. All peoples shall freely dispose of their wealth and natural resources. This right shall be exercised in the exclusive interest of the people. In no case shall a people be deprived of it.

2. In case of spoliation the dispossessed people shall have the right to the lawful recovery of its property as well as to an adequate compensation.

3. The free disposal of wealth and natural resources shall be exercised without prejudice to the obligation of promoting international economic cooperation based on mutual respect, equitable exchange and the principles of international law.

4. States parties to the present Charter shall individually and collectively exercise the right to free disposal of their wealth and natural resources with a view to strengthening African unity and solidarity.

5. States parties to the present Charter shall undertake to eliminate all forms of foreign economic exploitation particularly that practiced by international monopolies so as to enable their peoples to fully benefit from the advantages derived from their national resources.

A careful examination of this provision indicates that energy and water companies operating for example in Cameroon can be held accountable either directly or indirectly for any violation of the rights of the citizens.

[117] The European Convention [*on Human Rights?*] has 21 parties, while the American system [*Which one is that?*] covers 19 states.

2.3 Institutional Framework

Institutions with sectorial attributions refer to ministerial departments which have environmental issues to manage. Hardly is there a Ministry which can be said to be completely dissociated from environmental programs. Though involved at different levels, all Ministries are concerned with the environment. This is because the activities they manage either affect the environment directly or in a secondary manner. For the purpose of convenience, only a handful of Ministries having important environmental functions shall be selected and can be grouped into two, namely ;

- Those whose competences are completely focused on the management of environmental resources and its surroundings ; and
- Those whose intervention is based on the support of other ministries.

2.3.1 Ministry of Water and Energy Resources (MINEE)

This Ministry that used to be one was split into theMinistry of Water and Energy and the Ministry of Industry, Mines and Technological Development. The Ministry of Water and Energywas created byDecree N° 2005/087 of 29 March 2005 on the Organisation of the Ministry of Water and Energy. This Ministry has as its main function the elaboration, implementation and evaluation of government policy on the production, transportation and distribution of water and energy. To effectively accomplish this objective, the Ministry is in charge of :

- Elaborating government's strategic plan on the provision of water and energy ;
- Prospection, research and protection and exploitation of water in towns and rural areas
- Promotion of new energy in collaboration with the Ministry of in charge of Scientific Research.[118]

[118] Article 1(2) of Decree No.2005/087 of 29 March 2005 on the Organisation of the Ministry of Water and Energy.

Sub section 3 further provides that this ministerial body shall have the responsibility to monitor establishments and corporate bodies involved with the production, transportation, storage and distribution of Electricity, Gaz, Petrol and Water and also exercise same authority over the Société Camerounaise de Dépôts Pétroliers (SCDP).[119] It has supervisory authority over the national portable water distribution body, the former SNEC which is now CAMWATER.

Though it is clear that the activities of this Ministry do not directly involve environmental governance or environmental management, it can equally not be denied that these activities centres around natural resources, the exploitation of which affects the environment. Little wonder why the compliance and enforcement of corporate social responsibility in environmental governance features as one amongst the broad base activities of the Ministry. These activities are executed within the confines of the law regulating this sector.[120] These instruments place on the Minister of Water and Energy Resources the duty to ensure that proper provision is made for the environment through the supply of water for drainage, the safe disposal of sewage, effluents and water borne wastes, and the control and prevention of pollution[121] and also protection of inland and estuarine fisheries, flora and fauna.[122] This explains that the role of this Ministry vis a vis the enforcement and compliance to CSR in environmental governance in Cameroon cannot be undermined.

The central stakeholder role in the current institutional electricity framework in Cameroon is shaped by the Ministry for Water and Energy (MINEE).[123] Thus the recent decentralisation legislation decentralised local authorities as

---

[119] See Article 1(3), *ibid.*

[120] The regulations referred to are Law No. 98/005 of 14 April 1998, Laying down Regulations Governing Water Resources in Cameroon, Decree No. 2001/164/PM of 8th May 2001 Regulating the Utilization of Water Resources and Decree No. 2001/165/PM of 8th May 2001, on the Protection of Water Resources.

[121] *Op cit*, Section 4 (1).

[122] *Ibid.*

[123] Section 71, Electricity Law.

well as the privatisation policy have a particular impact on the governance of electricity management in Cameroon. In total three main groups of stakeholders compose the institutional electricity sector framework on the national level which are ;

i The state represented mainly by MINEE and additional ministries,
ii The public-private sector represented by ENEO,
iii The Financial and technical cooperation partners.

The above mentioned stakeholders do not include the civil society and NGOs as relevant stakeholders because its active participation power oner.
These establishment have gone a series or privitisation process. With regards to electricity, it is undisputable fact that is a national heritage, which the State has to protect and manage to ensure all citizens the access to electricity just as drinking water. Several rules were implemented to start the privatistion of the old state-owned water company SONEL, which was fostered by a series of three SAPs. Nearly twelve years after the privatisation of the former National Electricity Company of Cameroon (SONEL), bought by Americans AES Sirocco, AES National Electricity Corporation (AES-Sonel) was created July 18, 2001 after the concession of SONEL. Its mission is providing the largest number of Cameroonian reliable and clean energy, not only through the upgrade of existing electrical installations but mainly through the addition of new electrical connections.

Cameroon, during the presence of AES-SONEL had already significant resources to the development of hydropower. Its economically exploitable hydropower potential is estimated at 20,000 MW, mainly available in the Sanaga Basin, the country could produce much more energy if these resources were appropriately exploited. The development of hydropower takes place through major projects of dams and hydropower plants, some of which are already identified in the Development Plan of the Electricity Sector : reservoir dam at Lom Pangar ; Nachtigal, SongNdong, Song-Mbengue, Kikot and other plants on the Sanaga basin, the development of the Memve'ele power station in the Ntem Basin, the hydroelectric development of the Bini to strengthen the capacity of Northern hydroelectric Network, etc... The main purpose of the reservoirs was not only to maintain river flows but also to cover forecast in electricity demands.

With the coming of ENEO, It has three main hydro power plants which are Songloulou, Edea and Lagdo. In order to ensure constant supply of electricity, reservoir dams were built to back up the Songloulou and the Edea dams which is where the electricity generation takes place. Therefore the people of these local communities (surrounding these dams) expect the activities of ENEO to improve on their living standards and sustainable development in general. The primary objective of ENEO is to manage the public electricity service as a publis utility for the urban and rural areas in the entire country.

As concerns water, although both bottled water and tap water are destined for human consumption, they are regulated by the same state instituion which is the Ministry for Water and Energy (MINEE). In addition, the two kinds of water are legally regulated by the same pieces of legislations like the case with electricity but with specific legislation on water, namely ; Water Law.[124] Commercial Law with respect to its packaging and quality components which makes its saleable.

Tap water is regulated by the CamWater (*Camerounais des Eaux* (CDE)) under the authority of the Ministry of Water and Energy. This establishment has gone a series or privitisation process. The Cameroonian government stated in 1998 that water is a national heritage, which the state has to protect and manage to ensure all citizens the access to drinking water, at the same time several rules were implemented to start the privatization of the old state-owned water company SNEC, which was fostered by a series of three SAPs. The first attempt of privatisation in 1999, with Suez as private investor was declared as unsuccessful in 2003. Finally with the Decree No. 2005/494 of 30th December 2005 the new institutional framework was laid down and the restructured resulting in the creation of the public water company known as CamWater in 2005 by Decree No. 2005/493 &2005/494, 2005

[124] Law No. 98/005 of 14 April 1998.

and the private one Camerounais des Eaux (CDE) in 2007 covered its lease contract.

2.3.2 Ministry of Mines, Industry and Technological Development (MINMIDT)

The Ministry of Mines which was formally attached to the Ministry of Water and Energy is in charge of geological prospection and mineral activities and intellectual property rights. This Ministry plays a very important subsidiary role in environmental governance especially as its activities touch much on the extraction of natural resources and the environment, activities that are mostly performed by corporate institutions. This Ministry is in charge of the elaboration, and follow up of mining and industrial policy of the government and strategies for technological development in the different sectors of the national economy.[125] More specifically, the Ministry is amongst other things in charge of :

- Elaboration of the mining cartography ;
- Prospection of geographical and mining activities ;
- The valorisation of mining, petroleum and gaz resources ;
- Monitoring of the petroleum sector ;
- The promotion of home industries ;
- The development of industrial zones ;
- The promotion of investment in the mining industrial and technological sectors in collaboration with the administration concern ;
- The elaboration of the industrial plan of the country ;
- The local transformation of mining, agricultural and forestry products in collaboration with the Ministry of Agriculture and rural Development and the Ministry of Forestry and Wildlife and other administration involved.

[125] See article 2(2) of Decree No. 2012/432 of 1st October 2012, on the Organization of the Ministry of Mines, Industry and Technological Development.

This Ministry has supervisory authority over National Investment Corporation (SNI), the Norms and Quality Agency (ANOR), l'Agence de Promotion des Investissement (Apl) ; l'Office National des Zones Franches Industrielles (ONZFI), la Chambre de Commerce, d'Industrie, des Mines et de l'Artisanat (CCIMA) and la Mission d'Aménagement et de Gestion des Zones Industrielles (MAGZI).[126] The underlying message here is that the Ministry manages the exploitation of certain natural resources as stipulated above and this is done by corporate bodies duly issued the license to operate by the Ministry. These exploitation licences are usually granted with conditions that EIA be conducted, strict respect for environmental norms. The activities of these sectors seriously affect the environment, the reason why it is incumbent on the competent Ministry to, in collaboration with other sister ministries regulate the activities of these companies and take measures to ensure that companies respect the regulations in force. It is no news that, as provided by these texts, failure to respect these conditions may lead to sanctions ranging from warning, through fines, suspension of licence, withdrawal of licence to judicial action.

2.4 Conclusion

The chapter focussed on analyses of laws and regulations articulating environmental aspects of corporate social responsibility in environmental governance in Cameroon. These legal instruments include command and control regulations and voluntary approaches which are all schemes to enhance environmental governance. The analyses concentrated on the international and domestic legal framework on the subject matter under consideration. This is because most local legislations draw their inspiration from universally accepted legal principles. The domestic laws and regulations were analysed from two dimensions, with the former concentrating on regulations with general attribution while the latter focused on regulations with sectoral attributions. The analyses from both sections revealed that the Cameroonian legislator is conscious of the role companies play in environmental degradation

---

126 *Ibid*, Article 4.

and as such has attempted measures aimed at preventing and mitigating same through the imposition of corporate social responsibilities.

A cross section of the laws and regulations examined demonstrate uniformity in the responsibilities imposed on corporate bodies irrespective of the sectors the laws regulate. Frequent among these are : Environmental impact assessment, Corporate disclosure or reporting, Responsibility to mitigate environmental harm resulting from corporate activities and the duty to monitor. Even though these laws and regulations have been put in place to govern environmental activities in the country, there has been some degree of inefficacies and uncertainties in the laws that may turn to infringe on the proper implementation of the laws. The government of Cameroon has seen to this effect that, companies operating within the framework of its territory should make sure that their activities are in line with the available respective laws of the land. Having identified from the reading of the provisions of the laws and regulations that specific environmental responsibilities have been imposed by the legislator, it is worthwhile to establish of the raison d'être or necessity for a right to a healthy environmental as a component of corporate social responsibility in environmental governance in Cameroon. This is the purport of another chapter of this book.

CHAPTER THREE

THE RAISON D'ETRE FOR ENVIRONMENTAL GOVERNANCE

3.0 Introduction

The persistent efforts of Cameroon towards environmental governance indicates the clarity of the argument that development and environmental protection are not opposing concepts but rather, that environmental protection could only be a means to guarantee a long lasting development, what may be termed sustainable development. This new drift has since seen the introduction of several actors in the process of environmental governance. Corporations now seem to be recognising the potential competitive advantage to be gained by responding to stakeholder expectations for environmental performance of the company as a whole or of its product individually. Issues that many managers use to think are of little importance for business such as environment, diversity, human rights and community are now very important for business, they are hard to ignore, hard to manage and very hard for businesses that get them wrong.

Worth noting is the fact that the desire to engage corporate institutions in environmental governance through environmental responsibility through corporate social responsibility was guided amongst other things, by the willingness to adopt and comply with legal principles enshrined in international human rights and environmental conventions. Legal principles stem from international human rights and environmental conventions and some provide a framework for the development and convergence of national and sub-national environmental laws[127] which provides a basis for environmental protection at the national level. As Hunter et al.[128] Put it, 'even where principles or concepts have not yet become Customary Law, they can be used to put political pressure on states to apply these principles in domestic law'.

In Cameroon, commitments towards obliging corporate institutions to embrace corporate social responsibility took a serious stands in the late 1980s. The *raison d'être* for the sudden change of attitude in favour of environmental governance through the imposition of environmental responsibilities in corporate social responsibilities encompass the respect of Human Rights as enshrined in international and national human rights instruments, compliance to basic principles of international environmental law, ethical and moral principles and the desire to uphold traditional rules and cultural belief systems. This chapter therefore seeks to unravel the *raison d'être* or necessity for imposing environmental aspects of social responsibilities on companies operating on Cameroonian territory.

3.1 Respect for Human Rights under International and National Human Rights Law

The United Nations Charter[129] does not define human rights. However, the human right to environment could be interpreted through the concept of 'well-being'.[130] Similarly, the Universal Declaration of Human Rights (UDHR)[131] does not mention a human right to environment. It affirms the right to life and a right to a standard of living adequate for health and well-being. Again, the right to environment could be read into this right. Human oneribes however be defined as those rights which are inborn in man and are inalienable. They are the very essence of human existence and without them man cannot

[127] Hunter, D., Saizman, J., Zaelke, D., *International Environmental Law and Policy,* (Foundation Press 1998), New York, p. 320.
[128] *Ibid*, p. 321.
[129] The Charter of the United Nations, 1945.
[130] Dias A., Human Rights, Environment and Development: with Special Emphasis on Corporate Accountability, (2000), Human Development Report, Background Paper, p. 7.

exist. Over the past fifty years, international environmental law scholars and activists have increasingly looked to the law of human rights not only as a model for the progressive development of international environmental law, but as a potential independent tool for protecting the environment.[132] Many environmentalists now argue for the recognition of environmental rights, based on the fundamental human needs for clean air and water, a stable climate system and more generally the environment conducive to human life and health.[133] Yet, not all observers believe that the right-based approach would prove effective in dealing with the relatively complex and technical nature of global environmental issues.

Regardless of whether one favours a right-based approach to environmental protection, the field of human rights will remain vital for environmental protection and achieving sustainable development. Environmental and human rights issues necessarily converge. The link between human rights and environment raises a cluster of closely related questions : how are human rights and the environment related ; to what extent are environmental rights recognised in existing legal arrangements ; how are environmental rights defined, justified and applied ; and what are the advantages and disadvantages of approaching environmental issues through a human rights framework. The environmentally unfriendly behaviours of corporate institutions do not only adversely affect the environment but also result in violation of human rights. Environmental degradation is all too often resulting in serious human rights violations.

Environmental protection can thus be seen as a precondition for the respect of human rights. Considering environmental protection as a 'precondition to the exercise of fundamental human rights', for instance, has inherent risks because the alleged lack of these preconditions might be and has been used to deny human rights. Others view environmental protection not as a precondition for human rights, but as an integral part of their enjoyment.[134]

---

[131] Universal Declaration of Human Rights (UDHR) was adopted by the General Assembly on December 10, 1948.

[132] Hunter, D. et al, *op cit*, note 1, p. 1305.

[133] *Ibid*, p. 1305.

[134] *Op cit*, note 4, p. 4.

Upon closer inspection, the precise relationship between human rights and environmental protection is far from clear. The relationship may be conceived in two main ways.

First, environmental protection may be cast as a means to an end of fulfilling human rights standard.[135] Since degraded physical environments contribute directly to infringements of the human rights to life, health and livelihood, acts leading to environmental degradation may constitute an immediate violation of internationally recognised human rights. The creation of a reliable and effective system of environmental protection through the control of corporate conduct would help ensure the well-being of future generations as well as the survival of those persons, often including indigenous or economically marginalised groups[136], who depend immediately upon natural resources for their livelihood. In the second approach, the legal protection of human onerибe an effective means to achieving the ends of conservation and environmental protection. Thus, a full realisation of a broad spectrum of first and second generation rights would constitute a society and a political order in which claims for environmental protection are more likely to be respected.[137] There is therefore an enhanced complementary relationship between environmental responsibilities and promoting and protecting human rights.

Furthermore, a pertinent issue that has raised debate and a split between scholars is whether the right to environment should be procedural or substantive in character. One view holds that the right to environment should be purely procedural. Adherents of this view argue that there are a range of procedural rights at both international and domestic levels which are relevant to environmental protection.[138] These include the

[135] *Op cit*, note 1, p. 1308.

[136] Although there is no clear definition of the term "indigenous peoples". As a result, a certain number of criteria have emerged in the course of discussions in the Working Group on indigenous populations. Indigenous peoples are the descendants of the original inhabitants of territories since colonised by foreigners; they have distinct cultures which set them apart from the dominant society; many have, until comparatively recently, had a high degree of control over their development; indigenous peoples have a strong sense of self-identity. It is held that indigenous peoples have a special relationship with their land and the environment in which they live.

[137] Hunter, D. et al, *op cit*, note 1, p.1308.

[138] Dias, A., (2000), *op cit*, note 4, p. 9.

right to information, the right to receive prior notice of environmental risks, the right to participate in decision-making in environmental issues at both the domestic and international level, the right to environmental impact assessments, the right to legal remedies including standing to initiate public interest litigation and the right to effective remedies where environmental damage is caused.[139] A participatory approach leads to environmental protection. This is especially so where marginalised groups and communities who are affected can take part in decisions which concern them. Advocates of procedural rights add that, a single precise formulation of a substantive right to environment is not feasible since the desired quality of the environment is a value judgement which is difficult to codify in legal language.[140]

Conversely, proponents for a substantive right to environment posit that such a right would provide more effective protection. To them, a substantive right can provide more effective protection, and may play a role in defining and mobilising support for environmental issues. They see procedural rights as lacking, in the sense that, they cannot guard against a participatory and accountable polity that oneri for short-term affluence rather than long-term environmental protection. As such, procedures alone cannot guarantee environmental protection. Whether or not human rights to the environment should be substantive or procedural is not of the utmost importance here. What is interesting is the fact that a variety of environmental human rights have been incorporated in human rights instruments of both international and domestic coverage.

3.1.1 Rights under International Human Rights Instruments

Although a proposal to include a list of fundamental human rights in the United Nations Charter 1945 failed, the Charter nonetheless included as one of its purposes "*promoting and encouraging respect for human rights*

[139] See Alan E. Boyle and Michael R. Anderson, Human Rights Approaches to Environmental Protection (Oxford, OUP, 1996), p. 313.

[140] *Op cit*, note 12, p.10.

and for fundamental freedoms for all without distinction as to race, sex, language or religion".[141] With the adoption of the Universal Declaration of Human Rights (UDHR),[142] individuals for the first time became subjects of international law in their own albeit limited right. The body of human rights now comprises about twenty universal treaties, more than a dozen regional conventions and score of declarations, resolutions and soft law instruments. The first major UN human rights instrument was the non-binding UDHR, adopted as a UN General Assembly Resolution.[143] The Declaration was later followed by two human rights covenants adopted in1966.[144] The Americas, Europe and Africa have established regional human rights system. Each has at least one major declaration or convention and either a commission or court or both.

3.1.1.1. The Inter-American System.

In 1948, the ninth International Conference of American States adopted the American Declaration on Human Rights and Duties of Man. This was a non-binding declaration which was replaced in 1978 when the American Convention on Human Rights (Pact of San José, Costa Rica) entered into force.[145] Neither the American Convention nor the Declaration refers explicitly to the protection of the environment.

3.1.1.2 The European System.

The European Convention for the Protection of Human Rights and Fundamental Freedoms (hereinafter referred to as ECPHRFF)[146] created both the European Commission and the Court of Human Rights. The environment is not referred to in the European Convention. Nonetheless, the European

[141] See Art 1(3) of the Charter of the United Nations, 1945.
[142] The Universal Declaration of Human Rights, 1948 it should be noted, does not contain the third generation rights which inclusively includes environmental human rights.
[143] U.N.G.A. 217A (III) U.N.Doc.A/810 (Dec. 10, 1948).
[144] These were the International Covenant on Civil and Political Rights (ICCPR) and the International Covenant on Economic, Social and Cultural Rights (ICESCR).
[145] Hunter. D et al, *op cit*, note 1, p.1312.
[146] The European Convention for the Protection of Human Rights and Fundamental Freedoms was adopted in 1950 and entered into force in 1953.

Commission has had a long and involved history with environmental related cases.[147]

3.1.1.3 The African System.

The African Charter on Human and Peoples Rights (ACHPR) was adopted by the then Organisation of African Unity (OAU, today known as African Union) in 1982 and entered into force in 1986. The Charter enumerates the traditional list of civil and political rights, but also includes economic, social and cultural rights and more controversially, third generation rights of solidarity. Included in this last category, is an explicit right of peoples to "*a general satisfactory environment favourable to their development*".[148]

Today, the link between human rights and environmental protection is glaring and many human rights instruments have established environmental human rights which are incorporated in environmental instruments.

3.1.1.4 The Right to a Healthy Environment

As noted above, most important human rights treaties were concluded before the relationship between environment and human rights was established. Thus, most human rights treaties do not contain an explicit general right to a healthy environment. An exception is the African Charter on Human and Peoples' Rights.[149] The Charter was the first human rights treaty to expressly recognise the right of 'all peoples' to a 'satisfactory environment favourable to their development'. Article 24 of the Charter provides that : "*all people shall have the right to a general satisfactory environment favourable to their development*". Within Europe, the Organisation of Economic Cooperation and Development (OECD) has stated that a "decent" environment should be

---

[147] The Commission and the Court have dealt with environmental questions under Article 8 (Rights to Privacy) and under Article 1 (Right to property) of Protocol I. See e.g. *Lopez Ostra vs. Spain*, 20 E.H.R.R. 277, Series A, No. 303 (Dec. 9, 1994), the Court ruled that the applicant suffered health problems from the fumes of a tannery waste treatment plant operating a few meters away from her home.

[148] See generally Article 24 of the ACHPR, 1981.

[149] See the African Charter on Human and Peoples' Rights, 1981.

recognised as one of the fundamental human rights. A key question of course is whether these rights provide meaningful environmental protection. It will be noticed immediately that the right is to be enjoyed by 'all peoples', as opposed to 'every individual' who is the beneficiary of the civil and political and economic and social rights contained in the Charter. It has been suggested that 'all peoples' refer to the entire population of a party state rather than any particular ethnic or other group within a party state.[150] Does it mean, for example, that no complaint can be made that a state is violating article 24, unless the population as a whole is enjoying a less than satisfactory environment, rather than a particular segment of the population ?

Secondly, oneri be noted that the right to a satisfactory environment is linked to development. The meaning of this again is not clear. One may view it to mean that the focus of environmental measures should be those that will permit development to take place, such as the prevention of soil erosion and desertification, the provision of clean water, air contamination etc. No indication is given in the Charter as to what is meant by a 'general satisfactory environment' or the range of issues it might embrace. The expression of this right therefore raises many questions concerning its meaning and scope. This demonstrates the vague and laconic way in which much of the African Charter is drafted.

3.1.1.5 The Right to Life

The International Covenant on Civil and Political Rights (hereinafter referred to as ICCPR) and the International Covenant on Economic, Social and Cultural Rights (ICESPR) affirm that every human being has the "inherent right to life", and require states to protect that right by law. Thus, for example, Article 6(1) of the ICCPR states that : "*Every human being has the inherent right to life. This right shall be protected by law. No one shall be arbitrarily deprived of his life*".[151] It is clear that the right to life involves at least a prohibition on the state not to take life intentionally or negligently. Thus in

---

[150] Hunter, D. et al, *op cit*, note 1, p. 1317.

[151] The provisions contained in the European Convention and the American Convention are similar. See European Convention on the Protection of Human Rights and Fundamental Freedom (ECPHRFF), Art 2(1) and American Convention on Human Rights (ACHR), Art 4(1).

extreme cases the right may be invoked by individuals to obtain compensation where death resulted from some environmental disaster in so far as the state is responsible.[152] In environmental terms, the right to life may include a positive obligation on the state to take steps to prevent a reduction of or an extension of life expectancy. For example, by providing better drinking water or less polluted air.

The limited case law in this area usually deals with noise pollution for example, in alleged nuisance complaints about excessive aircraft noise at Heathrow Airport the European Court on Human Rights found that the benefits to the community out-weighed the individual's right to bring a claim.[153] However, in the case of *Lopez Ostra v Spain*,[154] the Court ruled that the applicant suffered health problems from the fumes of a tannery waste treatment plant operating a few meters away from her home. To sum up therefore, while the right to life appears to have some potential application to the environmental field, it has not yet been successfully invoked under the machinery for individual complaints provided for by these treaties.[155]

3.1.1.6 The Right to Health

In a series of resolutions between 1993 and 1995, the UN Commission on Human Rights concluded that the promotion of an environmentally healthy world contributes to the protection of the human rights to life and health

[152] See for example the Bhopal or Chernobyl incidents. The Bhopal disaster was an explosion at the Bhopal Union Carbide India Limited (UCIL) pesticide plant in India in 1984. It is still the world's most lethal industrial disaster. It is well established that in its immediate aftermath many thousands of people died as a result of the inhalation of toxic fumes. A large proportion of these deaths were probably due to acute respiratory damage. For Chernobyl, on April 26, 1986, a sudden surge of power during a reactor systems test destroyed Unit 4 of the nuclear power station at Chernobyl, Ukraine, in the former Soviet Union. The accident and the fire that followed released massive amounts of radioactive material into the environment.

[153] Dias A., *op cit*, note 4, p.8.

[154] *Lopez Ostra v. Spain*, 20 EHRR 277 of 9 December, 1994.

[155] A justification is the fact that in spite of the apparent potential for invoking the right to life to improve the environment, only two cases are known to have been brought under the complaints machinery of the treaties. First, under the covenant, a group of Canadian citizens alleged that the storage of radioactive wastes near their homes threatened the right to life of present and future generations in the area. The Human Rights Committee, while acknowledging that the case raised serious issues with regards to the obligations of states parties to protect human life, declared the application inadmissible for non-exhaustion of domestic remedies. (Communication No. 67/1980, *EHP vs. Canada*, 2 Selected Decisions of the Human Rights Committee, (1990), 20.

of everyone.[156] The commission equally called upon states to act on this in accordance with their common but differentiated responsibilities and respective capacities. Equally, the ICCPR and the ICESCR affirm the right of everyone to the enjoyment of the highest attainable standard of physical and mental health, through the improvement of all aspects of environmental and industrial hygiene.[157] Part 1 of the 1961 European Social Charter requires parties to take appropriate measures in particular to prevent air and water pollution, protection from radioactive substances, noise abatement, food control and environmental hygiene.[158] Similarly, the American Protocol to the Inter-American Convention on Human Rights provides that everyone shall have the right to health.[159]

Perhaps, the most striking is the Convention on the Rights of the Child, which provides that a child has the right to enjoy the highest attainable standard of health.[160] For the first time in any human rights treaty, there is an explicit link between health and the State of the environment.

3.1.1.7 The Right to Environmental Information

Access to environmental information is a prerequisite to public participation in decision making and to monitoring governmental and private sector activities. It also can assist private enterprises in planning for and utilising the best available techniques and technology. Human rights texts generally contain a right to information or a corresponding state duty to inform. This right is included in the UDHR.[161] The same right is also provided for by the ICCPR,[162] the ACHPR[163] and the African Charter on the Rights and Duties of Peoples.[164] European states are generally bound by article 10 of the European

---

[156] Hunter, D, *op cit*, note 1, p. 1321.

[157] See Article 12 of the ICESCR for complete provision. Also, Article 10 of the American Protocol to the American Convention on Human Rights, 1988.

[158] See also Article 11 of the European Social Charter, 1961.

[159] Article 10 of the American Protocol to the Inter-American Convention on Human Rights, 1988.

[160] Article 24 of the Convention on the Rights of the Child, 1989.

[161] Article 19 of the UDHR, provides that: "*Everyone has the right to freedom of opinion and expression; this right includes freedom to hold opinions without interference and to seek, receive and impart information and ideas through any media and regardless of frontiers*".

[162] Art 19(2) of the International Covenant on Civil and Political Rights, 1966.

[163] Article13, ICCPR, 1966.

[164] *Ibid*, Article 9.

Convention on Human Rights, which guarantees the freedom to receive information.

The nature of environmental deterioration which often arises only long after a project is completed and can be irreversible, compels early and complete data to make informed choices. Trans boundary impacts also produce significant demands for information across borders. A right to information can mean, narrowly, freedom to seek information, or, more broadly, a right to access to information, or even a right to receive it.[165]

To fully guarantee the protection of these rights, human rights to environment have been incorporated in many international and national environmental legal instruments of both binding and non-binding nature. Rio Principle 10 for instance, calls for states to provide environmental information. Similarly, Chapter 23 of Agenda 21, on strengthening the role of major groups, proclaims that individuals, groups and organisations should have access to information relevant to the environment and development, held by national authorities, including information on products that have or are likely to have a significant impact on the environment.[166]

3.1.2 Rights under National Human Rights Instruments

According to Ayesha[167], human rights norms, which are already protected under international instruments, play an important role in environmental protection. The author further acknowledges that the existing rights protected under international human rights instruments are sufficient to provide environmental protection and that to create new environmental rights would be superfluous and at worst counter-productive. The accuracy of this assertion may be questionable as the concept of sovereignty warrants that individual states take responsibility for managing the environment within their respective

---

[165] Kiss, A., Shelton, D., *International Environmental Law* (3rd ed., Transnational Publishers 2004), New York, p. 373.

[166] Similar provisions are made in Article 6 of the UNFCCC 1992, Article 13 & 14 of the Convention on Biological Diversity 1992, Article 10(1) of the Convention on Persistent Organic Pollutant, 2001, etc.

[167] Dias A., (2000), *op cit*, note 4, p.5.

territories. Increasingly though, these rights elaborated by the international instruments treated above, have been ratified and incorporated into national legal and policy frameworks of most countries.

The right to environment has found increasing recognition at the national level in several national constitutions and laws. To begin with Cameroon, the Preamble of the 1996 constitution[168] in a single statement provides certain basic environmental rights and obligations which must be observed. This Constitution provides that "*every person shall have a right to a healthy environment. The protection of the environment shall be the duty of every citizen. The State shall ensure the protection and improvement of the environment*".[169] As stated earlier, the burning issue remains whether the preamble is part and parcel of the Constitution as such that it is of any legal value as championed by the late professor Stanislas Melone and others[170] who aver that it is not an integral part of the Constitution and consequently, is devoid of any legal value. According to them, the preamble of the Constitution contains only general declarations that do not have the force. Opinions of both judicial and administrative judges have also divided on the legal value of the preamble. The 1996 revised Constitution however settles the debate as it provides that : "*the preamble shall be part and parcel of this Constitution*".[171] Since 1996, therefore, the provisions on environmental concerns are part and parcel of the Cameroonian Constitution.

Apart from Cameroon, the following are some examples of nations that have implemented a substantive right to environment within their domestic corpus of law. To begin with, The Portuguese Constitution in article 66 states that "*Everyone shall possess the right to a healthy and ecologically balanced human living environment and the duty to defend it*".[172] In

---

[168] Law No. 96/06 of 18 January 1996 on the Constitution of Cameroon.

[169] Paragraph 24 of the Preamble of Law No 96/06 of 18 January 1996 to amend the Constitution of 2 June 1972 (the Constitution of the Republic of Cameroon).

[170] For a detailed explanation of the position of Melone and others, see page 12-13 and foot note 33, chapter two of the current research.

[171] Section 65 of the 1996 Constitution.

[172] See Article 66(1) & (2) of Law No. 1/97 of 20 September 1997 on the Revised Constitution of Portugal.

the same vein,the Constitution of the Democratic Republic of Congo[173] in article 41 provides that "*each citizen shall have the right to healthy, satisfactory and enduring environment*".[174] Again, the Constitution of Brazil, Chapter VI, article 225 states "*all have the right to an ecologically balanced environment, which is an asset of common use and essential to a healthy quality of life, and both the Government and the community shall have the duty to defend and preserve it for present and future generations*".[175] These are just a few examples ; in fact over 60 countries as well as several sub-national governments (states) within the US have adopted similar provisions in their constitutions.

3.2 Compliance to Basic Principles of International Environmental Law

International law, as traditionally defined, governed relations among judicially equal states, once considered the sole subjects of international law.[176] International law has regulated interstate relations through rules based on the consent of states reflected in the adoption of treaties and the development of customary international law through state practice viewed as obligatory (opinion juris). While the contours of this classic system remained intact, it has undergone fundamental changes. International Environmental Law is both a product of and in part of a cause of this transformation that affects the process of law making and the role of consent as well as sovereignty. The field of international environmental law for the most part has not developed in any systematic or strategic way ; instead, it has developed ad hoc in response to specific environmental threats. As a result, the field consists of a large number of multilateral treaties, each addressing a different global or regional

[173] Article 41 of the Constitution of Democratic Republic of Congo, 25 October 2015.

[174] The original version of this Article is in French and providesthus: "*Tout citoyen a droit à un environnement sain, satisfaisant et durable et a le devoir de le défendre. L'Etat veille à la protection et à la conservation de l'environnement*".

[175] Chapter VI, article 225 of Constitutional text of October 5, 1988, with the alterations introduced by Constitutional Amendments No. 1/1992 through 64/2010 and by Revision Constitutional Amendments No. 1/1994 through 6/1994.

[176] Kiss, A., Shelton, D.,*Op cit*, note 39, p. 16.

environmental issue, and several general important soft law instruments[177] not intended to establish legally binding rules.

Despite the lack of any overarching instrument, a general framework for international environmental law can be stitched together from the concepts and principles that run through many international environmental instruments.[178] Since the Stockholm Declaration, much time has been spent, identifying, elaborating and developing basic concepts and principles in international environmental law. International environmental law has established numerous principles and states parties to these multilateral instruments are required to take cognisance and incorporate when drafting national environmental documents. These concepts and principles come from a wide variety of sources.[179]

Not surprising, given the wide range of sources for these principles and concepts and the relatively new and dynamic nature of international law making, the legal status of these principles varies. Some simply reflect the application of general international law principles to environmental issues specifically.[180] Others are now widely considered to be part of customary international environmental law.[181] Most of the other principles and concepts, however, probably cannot yet be viewed as customary international law. Some of them are supported by considerable state practice, while others have just recently begun to be implemented at the national level.[182]

Even so, these principles serve a number of other functions : firstly, some may provide a framework for negotiating new and existing agreements while others provide the rules of decision for resolving trans boundary

[177] The Stockholm Declaration 1972, the Rio Declarations 1992, the Johannesburg Declaration on Sustainable Development 2002.

[178] Hunter et al, *op cit*, note 1, p. 319.

[179] Some of these sources include soft law instruments, like the Rio Declaration; the UN General Assembly Resolutions; arbitral decisions like the Trial Smelter Arbitration; Judicial decisions of the International Court of Justice etc.

[180] Examples of these principles are the principles of good neighbourliness and the obligation to resolve disputes peacefully.

[181] Reference here is made particularly to the obligation not to cause environmental harm to areas outside national jurisdiction.

[182] Hunter, *loccit*, note 52, p. 319.

environmental disputes.[183] Again, some assist in the integration of international environmental law with other fields, yet others, most importantly, provide a framework for the development and convergence of international, national and sub national environmental laws.[184] These principles provide the bases for the imposition of corporate responsibility in environment governance under national environmental laws.

3.2.1 The Principle of Common Concern of Humankind

The cohesion of every society is based upon and maintained by a value system such as a common religion, culture, philosophy, ideology or ethics. The system may demand respect for the human person, propriety, patriotism, and respect for cultural values or adherence to a particular social order. The protection of such fundamental values is generally recognised as a common concern of the community and is ensured through law. This principle is to the effect that certain environmental activities have a direct negative effect on humankind irrespective of the jurisdiction where it is situated.

International environmental law lacks a constitutional text and central authority to determine the common concern of all humanity because states individually and jointly draft and adopt legal regulations governing international relations.[185] During the second half of the twentieth century, states aimed to create a universal political organisation to maintain international peace and security and improve the wellbeing of all humanity.[186] This ambitious effort could only proceed by defining domains of common

[183] Assume a situation where one is asked to represent Cameroon in a dispute over the sitting of a hazardous waste facility in the Federal Republic of Nigeria just few kilometres from the border and scientists reports shows that both the air emissions and wastes discharges from the facility will harm Cameroon's environment. In the absence of any treaty, some of the principles place obligations on inter-state relations involving trans-boundary environmental disputes. In this respect, some of the principles may already be customary law, while others undoubtedly still emerging.

[184] Assume for instance that one is asked to provide comments on a draft environmental law of Cameroon, what internationally accepted principle, perhaps emanating from instruments signed by Cameroon, could one suggest be included in the national law? Even when principles or concepts have not yet become customary law, they can guide state practice in ways that tend to harmonise standards and practice. The elaboration of these principles often furthers the study of state practice in ways that can help promote the development of customary law.

[185] Kiss, A., Shelton, (2004), *op. cit*, note 39, p. 17.

[186] *Ibid.*

concern. The international recognition of human rights and fundamental freedoms constituted the first step of paramount importance in developing the concept of an international community built upon the fundamental values of humanity. Similarly, knowledge that the biosphere is the only known place in the universe where life is possible, led to the emergence of another universal value, protection of the human environment as a common concern of humanity. The global environment, an interdependent ecological system, can only be protected at the global level, making it a common concern for all humanity.

The concept of common concern of humankind has not been widely accepted when it comes to resources or activities located within countries. At the same time, a growing consensus has emerged that the planet is ecologically interdependent and that humanity may have a collective interest (based on environmental concerns) in certain activities that take place or resources that are located wholly within state boundaries. The compromise reached with respect to Biological Diversity Convention[187] and the Climate Change Convention[188] is that, they address "common concerns" of humankind. Thus, for example, the Biodiversity Convention affirms that "*the conservation of biological diversity is a common concern of humankind*",[189] even though most biodiversity is found within individual member states. Similarly, the UNFCCC acknowledges that "*change in the earth's climate and its adverse effects are a common concern of humankind*"[190]

Although the principle was first used in the environmental context in 1992 biodiversity and climate change conventions, all international environmental treaties and instruments arguably reflect a growing acceptance that protecting the environment and achieving sustainable development generally are common concerns of humanity. States are thus required to reflect this principle when drafting and enacting national

---

[187] The Convention on Biological Diversity (CBD), adopted May 22, 1992, opened for signature June 5, 1992, in force December 29, 1993.
[188] The United Nations Framework Convention on Climate Change (UNFCCC), 1992.
[189] See the Preamble of the CBD, *loccit*,note 61.
[190] The Preamble of the United Nations Framework Convention on Climate Change, 1992.

environmental texts. The onus of preventing and controlling environmental activities that would adversely affect humanity is placed on states. Since unregulated corporate environmental behaviours negatively affect the environment and the climate in particular and in keeping with the principle of common concern of humanity, there was the need to check corporate conduct by creating and imposing responsibilities to this effect. Today, almost all national constitutions proclaim fundamental rights and require the government to respect and ensure those rights. Increasingly, similar provisions are included in the same text and other national environmental instruments. Article 66 of the 1976 Portuguese Constitution for example is illustrative.[191] In Cameroon, a panoply of legislation has been enacted to that effect.

3.2.2 Obligation not to cause Environmental Harm

The obligation of states not to cause harm to the environment is a central principle in international environmental law. This principle has been elaborated in portions of international environmental soft law instruments. The Stockholm Declaration for instance, states that :

> States have in accordance with the Charter of the United Nations and the principles of international law, the sovereign right to exploit their own resources pursuant to their own environmental and developmental policies, and the responsibility to ensure that activities within their jurisdiction or control do not cause damage to the environment of other states or of areas beyond the limits of national jurisdiction.[192]

The phrase "areas beyond the limits of national jurisdiction" includes for example, oceans and Antarctica. This principle seems to prohibit only the

---

[191] It proclaims an obligation on the state through its agencies to prevent and control pollution and its effects and harmful forms of erosions, to organise territorial space so as to establish biologically balanced landscapes and to create national parks and reserves.

[192] Principle 21 of the Stockholm Declaration on Human Environment, 1972. The same is provided by Principle 2 of the Rio Declaration on the Environment and Development, 1992.

impacts from activities under a state's jurisdiction or control.[193] Further emphasis on this principle has been made in arbitral decisions and most recently in the advisory opinion of the International Court of Justice (ICJ), regarding the legality of nuclear weapons.[194] The contours of this principle, probably more than any other, will determine the legal rights and responsibilities regarding international environmental damage and can be considered as part of customary international law.[195]

The obligation not to cause environmental harm has its roots in the common law principle of *sic uteretuoutalienum non laedus* which means that "one should not use his property to harm another". In the context of international law, states are under a general obligation not to use their territory, or to allow their territory to be used, in a way that can harm the interest of another state. The obligation not to cause harm to other states was extended to environmental damage in the well-known *Trial Smelter* Arbitration.[196] In its opinion on the decision of the tribunal after the two countries agreed to arbitration, the US-Canada International Joint Commission stated that :

> The Tribunal, therefore, finds that the above decisions, taken as a whole, constitutes an adequate basis for its conclusions, namely, that, under the principles of international law, as well as of the law of the United States, no state has the right to use or permit the use of its territory in such a manner as to cause injury by fumes in or to the territory of another or the properties or the persons therein, when the case was of serious consequence and the injury is established by clear and convincing evidence.[197]

[193] See also Principle 2 of the Rio Declaration on the Environment and Development, 1992; Lac LanouxAbitration, (Spain v. France) XII R.I.A.A. 281 (1957); UNEP Principles for Shared Natural Resources, Principle 3; United Nations Convention on the Law of the Sea, Part XII; Article 11 of the IUCN Draft Covenant on Environment and Development.

[194] The Court handed down its advisory opinion on the 8 of July 1996, on the request made by the General Assembly of the United Nations on the question concerning the Legality of the Threat or Use of Nuclear Weapons

[195] Hunter et al, *op cit*, note 1, p.345.

[196] This was a case between the United States of America vs. Canada. In that case, fumes from a Canadian smelter were damaging U.S. citizens and property.

[197] Hunter et al, *loccit*, note 69, p. 346.

The *Trial Smelter* Arbitration however, technically provide little legal precedent (because the parties had agreed to a closely circumscribed arbitration proceeding), but the general obligation not to cause harm has been confirmed in several rulings of the ICJ. In the *Corfu Channel* case[198], the ICJ, while holding Albania responsible, acknowledged that the laying of the minefield which caused the explosions on October 22nd, 1946, could not have been accomplished without the knowledge of the Albanian government. The obligations resulting for Albania from this knowledge are not disputed between the parties. If Albania had been informed of the operation before the accidents of October 22nd, and in time to warn the British vessels and shipping in general of the existence of the mines in the *Corfu Channel*, her responsibility would be involved. The obligations incumbent upon the Albanian authorities consisted in notifying, for the benefit of shipping in general, the existence of a minefield in Albanian territorial waters and in warning the approaching British warships of the imminent danger to which the minefield exposed them.[199] Unfortunately, Albania neither notified the existence of the minefield nor warned the British warships of the danger they were approaching.

In fact, nothing was attempted by the Albanian authorities to prevent the disaster. This grave omission involved the international responsibility of Albania. The court therefore concluded that Albania was responsible under international law for the explosions which occurred in October 22nd and for the damage and loss of human life which resulted from them.

Most commentators assumed that principle 21 of the Stockholm Declaration reflected customary international law as supported by *Trial Smelter* and

[198] Corfu Channel Case, case between United Kingdom vs. Albania, Judgement of April 9th, 1949, ICJ Reports 1949, p. 4. This case concerned the damage to British warships caused by mines placed in Albanian waters.

[199] It should be noted that such obligations are based not on the Hague Convention of 1907, which is applicable in time of war, but on certain general and well recognised principles, namely: elementary considerations of humanity, even more exacting in peace than in war; the principle of freedom of maritime communication; and every states obligation not to allow knowingly its territory to be used for acts contrary to the rights of other states.

Corfu Channel. Until 1996, the ICJ, however, had never clearly confirmed that environmental interests were among those interests that should not be harmed by a state.[200] In an advisory opinion on the legality of the threat or use of nuclear weapons[201] in 1996, and focussing its analysis primarily on treaties relating to the environment, the court noted that it recognised that environment is under daily threats and that the use of weapons could constitute a catastrophe for the environment. The court further recognised that the environment is not an abstraction but represents the living space, the quality of life and the very health of human beings, including generations unborn. Thus, the existence of the general obligation of states to ensure that activities within their jurisdiction and control respect the environment of other states or of areas beyond national control is now a part of the corpus of international law relating to the environment.

Because this obligation not to harm the environment of other states and to respect the environment of other states as noted by the ICJ reflects customary law, states will be held responsible for transgressions of the principle.[202] States are therefore endowed with the obligation to make sure this principle is observed within their respective jurisdictions.

3.2.3 The Principle of State Responsibility

Under this principle, states are generally responsible for breaches of their obligations under international law. International tribunals have on several occasions affirmed the role of state responsibility. In the *factory of Chorzorcase,*[203] for example, the Permanent Court of International Justice (PCIJ), the predecessor of the ICJ, held that : "*It is a principle of international law and even a general conception of law, that any breach of an agreement*

[200] *Corfu Channel (U.K.v. Alb.),* Merits, 1949 I.C.J. Rep. 4, 22-23 (Judgement of April 9).

[201] This opinion was expressed in a portion gathering eleven to fourteen votes, and the courts found that customary and conventional international law neither expressly authorise nor expressly prohibit the use of nuclear weapons.

[202] It is worth noting however that o apply the principle requires detail answers to several significant issues, including, for example, what level of harm should trigger the obligation; to what standard of care should the state be held; what activities should be considered under the jurisdiction and control of the state; what remedies should be available to States who suffer such damage.

[203] PCJI, (1928), Ser.A, no. 17, p. 29, Case between Germany vs. Poland.

involves an obligation to make reparation".[204] It should be noted that the court had earlier stated that reparation is the indispensable complement of a failure to apply a convention, and there is no necessity for it to be stated in the convention itself.

In the same line, the *Corfu Channel* case discussed above further affirmed the state responsibility principle. The court found that for Albania to have allowed its waters to be mined, constituted a breach of its international obligation to ensure that its territory was not used in a way that harmed others. Relying on this ground and finding that Albania failed to take necessary steps to warn ships approaching the danger zone or to otherwise avoid the harm caused by exploding mines, the court concluded that Albania was "responsible under international law" for the explosions and was required to pay compensation for the loss of human life and property.

To demonstrate the value attached to the environment, in recent times, state responsibility has been extended to breaches of international environmental law as well. Thus, for example, states are responsible for breaching the obligation not to cause environmental harm. As noted above, both principles 21 and 2 of the Stockholm and Rio Declarations respectively refer to the responsibility of states to ensure that activities within their jurisdiction or control do not cause damage to the environment. Many commentators thus refer to both provisions as elaborating the principle of 'state responsibility for environmental harm'.[205] Nonetheless, it is useful to think of the 'obligation not to cause environmental harm' separately from the principle of 'state responsibility'. The latter is broader and applies to violations of all obligations under international law, such as breaches of the obligation to notify or consult, and not only for environmental harm as is the case with the former.

---

[204] Hunter et al, *op cit*, note 1, p. 351.
[205] *Ibid.*

3.2.4 The Principle of Intergenerational Equity

Protecting the global environment and sustainable development requires a long term view.[206] Interest in survival of the human species requires that humanity be seen to include not only present but also future generations. Concern for future generations can thus be seen as implicit in all that touches environmental protection, and the preservation of natural resources, reflected in the requirement that development be sustainable. This focus on future generations as a rightful beneficiary of environmental protection has led to the principle of intergenerational equity. In essence, the principle is one of fairness, that present generations should not leave future generations worse off by the choices they make today regarding the environment. Intergenerational equity requires that the present generations take into consideration the impact of its activities on future generations, giving them a seat on the table in making current decisions.[207] The importance of intergenerational equity can be demonstrated by the assertion that we did not inherit the world from our parents ; we borrowed it for our children.

International environmental texts have referred to the need to conserve the natural heritage of humankind for the benefit of present and future generations, at least since the Stockholm Declaration. The Declaration notes in its preamble that to defend and improve the human environment for present and future generations has become an imperative goal of humankind. Principle 1 states inter alia that : "*man.....bears a solemn responsibility to protect and improve the environment for present and future generations*".[208] Furthermore, Principle 2 endorsed a concern with future generations, stating :

> The natural resources of the earth, including the air, water, and flora and fauna and especially representative samples of natural

[206] The concept of sustainable development has been defined in many ways, but the most frequently quoted is from Our Common Future, also known as the Brundtland's Report. This report is entitled "Sustainable Development: Our Common Future", (1987), World Commission on Environment and Development (WCED), p. 43. The report refers to sustainable development as meeting the needs of the present generations without sacrificing the needs of future generations.
[207] Hunter et al, *op cit*, note 1, p. 355.
[208] Principle 1 of the Stockholm Declaration on the Human Environment 1972.

ecosystems, must be safeguarded for the benefit of present and future generations through careful planning or management, as appropriate.[209]

In the same year, the UNESCO World Heritage Convention included a reference to future generations.[210] Particularly significant is Article 3(1) of the Framework Convention on Climate Change which declares that : "*the parties should protect the climate system for the benefit of present and future generations of humankind*".[211] At the same time, Principle 3 of the Rio Declaration on the Environment and Development links concern for future generations with the right to development, declaring that the right to development must be fulfilled so as to equitably meet developmental and environmental needs of present and future generations.[212]

In fact, implementing this principle requires using natural resources sustainably and avoiding environmental damage that is irreversible. The importance of intergenerational equity can be seen in climate change. Because of the long lag-time between when greenhouse gas emissions occur and when they are naturally removed from the atmosphere (measured in decades to centuries, depending on the gas), decisions made today to reduce the emissions will have profound impacts on the quality of life 100 years later. Similarly, investments made today in researching and developing environmentally sustainable energy sources also constrain the energy choices available to future generations. On the basis of the treaty provisions, declarations and resolutions, it is possible to say that each generation may benefit from and develop the natural and cultural patrimony inherited from

[209] *Ibid*, Principle 2.

[210] Other recent texts mentioning future generations include the 1973 Convention on International Trade in Endangered Species of Wild Fauna and Flora; 1977 Convention on the Prohibition of Military or any other Hostile use of Environmental Modification Techniques; 1979 Convention on the Conservation of Migratory Species of Wild Animals; 1992 Convention on Biological Diversity and 1994 United Nations Convention to Combat Desertification to name but these. The same concept appears in United Nations General Assembly Resolutions. See, e.g., global climate for present and future generations of mankind , G.A. Res. 43/53, Dec. 6, 1988, U.N. Doc. A/Res/43/53 of 27/1/1989.

[211] For full details, see Article 3(1) of the UNFCCC, 1992.

[212] See Principle 3 of the Rio Declaration on Environment and Development, 1992.

previous generations, but then must pass it on to future generations in no worse condition than it was received.

A recognition of the rights of future generations raises the problem of defining a generation and means of implementing such rights. The concept of a generation is not clear. Based on the average life expectancy and reproductive patterns, time span of a human generation has been taken to be thirty years, but there are significant differences in both of these elements between individuals and between industrialised and developing countries.[213] In reality, there are no distinct generations, because at each moment hundreds of human beings are born and die. In law, therefore, it is perhaps more logical to speak of future humanity, rather than future generations, as the holder of rights and to recognise humanity, including its present and future members as a collective legal person. National and international law has already recognised various entities as legal persons, from the state and other levels of government to corporations. The same capacity could be afforded humanity as a whole, although this does raises the problem of who might represent it.

Whether the right word to employ is future generation or future humanity, it is undeniable that states are making efforts to ensure respect of this principle and to protect the generations yet unborn. Today, many national environmental legal texts and policy frameworks have calved out provisions intended to protect and control environmentally unfriendly activities within their jurisdiction, especially corporate polluting activities.

3.2.5 The Preventive Principle

Experience and scientific expertise will demonstrate that prevention should be the Golden Rule for the environment, for both ecological and economic reasons. This principle is a reflection of the popular adage that "*prevention is better than cure*". It is frequently impossible to remedy environmental injury : the extinction of species of fauna and flora, erosion and the dumping of persistent pollutants into the sea creates irreversible situations. Even when

[213] Kiss, A. at al, *op cit*, note 39, p.12.

harm can be remedied, the costs of rehabilitation are often prohibitive. The duty of prevention also clearly emerges from the international responsibility not to cause significant damage to the environment extra-territorially, but also, it seeks to avoid harm irrespective of whether or not there are trans-boundary impacts.[214] Occasionally referred to in the pollution context as the pollution prevention principle, the principle reflects the fact that protection of the environment is best achieved by preventing environmental harm in the first place rather than by attempting to remedy or compensate for such harm after it has occurred. As a guiding principle for international negotiations and national implementation, the prevention principle gives preference to environmental management policies that eliminate and reduce pollution before it occurs.

The principle is most developed at the international level with respect to pollution. The Stockholm Declaration sets out the principle in sweeping terms, stating that :

> The discharge of toxic substance or of other substances and the release of heat, in such quantities or concentrations as to exceed the capacity of the environment to render them harmless, must be halted in order to ensure that serious or irreversible damage is not inflicted upon ecosystems. [215]

The urge and preference for clean production method as desired by the principle has begun to appear in international environmental hard law instruments.[216] The requirement for prevention is complex owing to the

---

[214] *Ibid*, p. 113.

[215] Principle 6, Stockholm Declaration on the Human Environment, 1972.

[216] Article 4(3)(f) of the Bamako Convention on the Ban of the Import into Africa and the Control of Trans-boundary Movement and Management of Hazardous Wastes within Africa, 1991, for example, requires that: "*each party shall strive to adopt and implement the preventive, precautionary approach to pollution problems which entails, inter alia, preventing the release into the environment of substance which may cause harm tohumans or the environment without waiting for scientific proof regarding such harm. The parties shall co-operate with each other in taking the appropriate measures to implement the precautionary principle to pollution prevention through application of clean production methods, rather than the pursuit of a permissible emissions approach based on assimilative capacity assumptions*".

number and diversity of the legal instruments in which it occurs. Perhaps it can better be considered an overarching aim that gives rise to a multitude of legal mechanisms, including prior assessment of environmental harm,[217] licensing or authorisations that set out the conditions for operation and the consequences for violation of the conditions. Emission limits and other product or process standards, the use of best available techniques can all be seen as applications of the principle of prevention.

The primary obligation that seems to flow from the principle of prevention is prior assessment of potentially harmful activities.[218] Since the failure to exercise due diligence to prevent significant trans-boundary harm can lead to international responsibility, it may be considered that properly done environmental impact assessment can serve as one standard for determining whether or not due diligence was exercised. Preventive mechanisms also include monitoring, notification and exchange of information, all of which are general obligations in nearly all environmental agreements. In fact, the objective of almost all international environmental instruments is to prevent environmental deterioration, whether they concern pollution of the sea, inland waters, the atmosphere or the protection of living resources.

The preventive approach requires each state to exercise due diligence, which means to act reasonably and in good faith and to regulate public and private activities subject to its jurisdiction or control that are possibly harmful to any part of the environment. Suffice to note however that, the principle does not impose an absolute duty to prevent all harm, but rather an obligation on each state to prohibit activities that could cause significant damage to the environment, for instance the dumping of toxic waste into rivers or habitable environments. The state should equally regulate to minimise the detrimental

[217] Otherwise referred to as Environmental Impact Assessment.

[218] This duty is expressed in the Rio tests: Principle 17, Chapter 22 of Agenda 21, and Article 8(h) on the statement on forests. Article 14(1)(a) and (b) of the Biodiversity Convention treat both the national and the international aspects of the issue. See also, Art. 206 Convention on the Law of the Sea, Dec. 10, 1982 which is to the effect that, "*when states have reasonable grounds for believing that planned activities under their jurisdiction or control may cause substantial pollution of or significant and harmful changes to the marine environment, they shall, as far as practicable, assess the potential effects of such activities on the marine environment and shall communicate reports of the results of such assessments*".

consequences of permissible activities, by imposing limits and treatment measures and procedures.

The concept of prevention is partly linked to the notion of deterrence and the idea that disincentives such as penalties and civil liability will cause actors to take greater care in their behaviour to avoid the increased cost. Little empirical work has been done, but there is some evidence for the preventive effect of the liability regime. A study[219] examined the relationship between the imposition of strict liability for environmental damages and emissions of toxic chemicals into the environment and found that strict liability has little obvious effects on annual emission levels. This principle has been incorporated into national laws. The most prominent is the 1996 Law on Environmental Management in Cameroon, taking the appellation 'the principle of preventive action and correction (through priority at the source) of threats to the environment by using the best available techniques at an economically acceptable cost'.[220] It is of no gain therefore to say that the regulation and control of corporate activities (imposition of corporate responsibilities) on the environment is not motivated by the principle of prevention and to a wider perspective, to prevent environmental deterioration.

3.2.6 The Precautionary Principle

Most environmental issues involve complex analyses of scientific, technical and economic factors. The precautionary principle as such evolved from the recognition that scientific certainty often comes too late to design effective legal and policy responses for preventing potential environmental threats. Most often, there is rarely anything approximating perfect knowledge when law-makers are asked to make decisions whether to respond to a specific threat. The precautionary principle is one of the most important principles for anticipating and avoiding environmental damage before it occurs and thus it

[219] Austin, D., and Alberini, A., *An Analysis of the Preventive Effect of Environmental Liability: Environmental Liability, Location and Emissions Substitution, Evidence from the Toxic Release Inventory*, (Resource for the Future, Washington DC 2001), cited in Kiss, A. et al, op cit, note 39, p. 114.

[220] See Article 9(b) of Law No. 96/12 of 5th August 1996 relating to Environmental Management in Cameroon.

can lower the overall cost of mitigating or adapting to environmental damage. This principle is closely related to the principle of prevention because both are concerned with taking anticipatory actions to avoid environmental harm before it occurs. Precaution means preparing for potential, uncertain threats, when there is no irrefutable proof that damage will occur. It is prevention based on probabilities or contingencies but it cannot involve eliminating all claimed risks, even those without any basis, such as astrological predictions. The problems of irreversibility and scientific uncertainty are thus brought into international law. In essence, unlike the others, the precautionary principle transfers the burden of scientific proof necessary for triggering policy responses from those who support prohibiting or reducing a potentially offending activity to those who want to continue the activity.[221]

In highlighting the precautionary principle, the Rio Declaration elaborates that, where there are threats of serious or irreversible damage, lack of full scientific certainty shall not be used as a reason for postponing cost-effective measures to prevent environmental degradation.[222] In the *Southern Bluefin TunaCase*,[223] the International Tribunal on the Law of the Sea (ITLOS) seemed to view the precautionary principle more favourably than other tribunals. ITLOS could not conclusively assess the scientific evidence

[221] Kiss, A. et al, *op cit*, note 39, p. 360.

[222] Principle 15 of the Rio Declaration on Environment and Development 1992. The principle in slightly different formulations has been included in many international environmental instruments. See, e.g., the Catagena Protocol to the Convention on Biological Diversity is based upon the precautionary principle. It is contained in Article 1 on the objectives of the protocol which refers explicitly to Rio Principle 15. Articles 10 and 11 contain the key provisions on the principle. Article 10(6) says that: "*lack of scientific certainty due to insufficient relevant information and knowledge regarding the extent of the potential adverse effects of Living Modified Organism (LMO) shall not prevent the party from taking a decision on the LMO in order to avoid or minimise such potential adverse effects*". Others are, World Charter for Nature, Principle 11, G.A. Res. 37/7 (Oct. 28, 1982); Preamble of the Biodiversity Convention; Article 3.3 of the UNFCCC; Agenda 21, Para. 18.40(b) (iv), (1982). See also Cameron, J., and Abouchar, J, 'The Precautionary Principle: A Fundamental Principle of Law and Policy for the Protection of the Global Environment', (1991), 14 B.C. INT'L & COMP. L. Rev. 1, 2; Gundling. L, the Status in International Law of the Principle of Precautionary Action, (1990), 5 Int'L J. of Estuarine and Coastal L, 23, 26.

[223] Case between Australia and New Zealand vs. Japan.On 27 August 1999, the International Tribunal for the Law of the Sea, in a dispute between Australia, New Zealand and Japan, requested the parties immediately to refrain from conducting an experimental fishing programme (EFP) of Southern Bluefin Tuna (SBT), which in fact Japan had undertaken unilaterally. Reports of International Arbitral Awards Southern Bluefin Tuna (New Zealand-Japan, Australia-Japan), 4 August 2000, Volume XXIII p.1-57.

regarding the provisional measures sought by New Zealand and indeed, the latter requested the measures on the bases of the precautionary principle, pending a final settlement of the case.[224] ITLOS found that in the face of scientific uncertainty regarding the measures, action should be taken as a measure of urgency to avoid further deterioration of the tuna stock. This principle strictly speaking, does not provide much guidance on what actions to take, except to limit them to cost-effective measures, but rather on when to take them and based on what scientific evidence. The threshold inquiry is thus how serious a problem must potentially be and how well it is understood before the principle is applied. The principle should therefore have particular relevance in cases of serious or irreversible harm, such as toxic or industrial pollution and species extinction.

At the national level, this principle has sufficiently been transplanted in local instruments. In Cameroon for example, Article 9(a) of Chapter III entitled fundamental principles states that : "*the principle of precaution, according to which lack of certainty, given the current scientific and technical knowledge, should not retard the adoption of effective and commensurate measures aimed at preventing a risk entailing serious and irreversible damages for the environment at an economically acceptable cost*".[225] The law does not however define what economically acceptable cost is.

3.3 Ethical and Moral Principles

Another important reason why the environment should be of concern to industry relates to the moral and ethical dilemmas facing society. According to Rossouw[226], "*Ethics concerns itself with what is good or right in human interaction*". Ethical and moral concepts are grounded in deep ecological thinking as well as the beliefs and values of societies over the years. For

[224] Kiss, A et al, *op cit*, note 39, p. 117.

[225] Article 9(a), Environmental Law. .

[226] Rossouw, D., *Business Ethics in Africa* (2nd ed, Cape Town: Oxford University Press 2002), cited in Goosen, Xenia, Institutionalising ethics in organisations: The role of mentorship, (M.Phil Thesis, Rand Afrikaans University 2004), South Africa, 155 at p.3.

example, a traditional/indigenous form of the principle of trusteeship is reflected in an Ijaw[227] proverb this way :

"*We did not inherit the world from our fathers. We borrowed it for our children*".[228]

This reflects the idea of sustaining the resources of the earth for future generations also. It is grounded in deep cultural values and respect for the rights of future societies to meet their own needs. This concept is very much related to the principle of trusteeship of earth resources ; the first principle of modern environmental law[229] which argues that ownership of earth resources is only to be held in trust by existing human societies for future generations. It therefore makes it incumbent on current generations to use it wisely, manage it and take custody of it for future generations.[230] Closely related to this principle is the "respect-for-nature" principle which postulates that the earth and its resources have intrinsic rights to exist without being exploited.[231] This principle pushes further the view that the existence of the earth and its resources should be independent of the uses and benefits to be derived from it by man. Arguing from this philosophical perspective therefore, the environment is viewed metaphorically as a stakeholder incorporate sustainability and hence is factored in, in the stakeholder value centred model of business mandate. The role of humans therefore is to understand and work with the rest of nature, not oneribes (what may be termed as the principle of cooperation).[232]

Earlier, Goodpaster and Mathews[233] made a succinct case for the environment and other social ends by arguing that corporations collectively should

---

[227] The Ijaw people are a tribe living in the modern day country of Nigeria.

[228] Nukpezah Daniel, Corporate Environmental Governance in Ghana: Studies on Industrial Level Environmental Performance in Manufacturing and Mining, (PhD Thesis, Brandenburg University of Technology, Cottbus 2010), p. 27. (Unpublished).

[229] Hunter et al, *op cit*, note 1, p. 358.

[230] Worthy of note here is the fact that this concept again raises the worry of identification and classification of generations.

[231] Miller, G.T., *Living in the environment*, (Wadsworth Publishing Co. 1990), Belmont, CA, USA, cited in Nukpezah, *op cit*, note 102, p. 27.

[232] Nukpezah, *op cit*, note 102, p.27.

[233] Goodpaster, Kenneth E., *Conscience and Corporate Culture*, (Malden, Massachusetts: Blackwell Publishing, 2007).

possess a moral conscience towards them. Since laws are chiefly reactionary, corporations should be seen to be proactive in reducing pollution burden on the environment and using resources sustainably even if there are no laws enforcing compliance.[234] This current study brings on board the extent to which these concepts are reflected (through voluntary actions) in national environmental laws and corporate environmental actions of companies in Cameroon. Indeed Vazquez and Liston-Heyes[235] show with an empirical study that corporate discourse (in the form of mission statements and corporate philosophies) affects the corporate mindset and correlates positively with corporate environmental performance.

All the concepts discussed above form part of the foundational basis for corporate social responsibility in environmental governance and provides legal, theoretical and philosophical basis for corporate environmental governance which is analysed in this dissertation.

3.4 Traditional Rules and Cultural Belief Systems

Since time immemorial, conservation of natural resources has been an integral part of diverse cultures in different ways. The traditional worship practices show the symbiotic relation of human beings and nature.[236] Indigenous communities all over the world lived in harmony with nature and valuable biodiversity. Ancestral knowledge and history holds that many traditional communities, forest dwellers, and subsistence hunting and farming communities have long engaged in sustainable practices and developed unique knowledge about their environments and their resources.[237] In addition, many

[234] *Ibid.*

[235] Vazquez, D.A. and Liston-Heyes C., Corporate Discourse and Environmental Performance in Argentina, (2008), Business Strategy and the Environment 17:179-193.

[236] Rim-Rukeh A., Irerhievwie G., Agbozu I.E., "Traditional beliefs and conservation of natural resources: Evidences from selected communities in Delta State, Nigeria", (2013), International Journal of Biodiversity and Conservation, Vol. 5(7), p. 426-432, available at http://www.academicjournals.org/IJBC, (accessed 2/07/2016).

[237] Sarfo-Mensah Paul, and Oduro William, 'Traditional Natural Resources Management Practices and Biodiversity Conservation in Ghana: A Review of Local Concepts and Issues on Change and Sustainability', (2007), FondazioneEni Enrico Mattei Working Paper Series, NOTA DI LAVORO 90, 1-14, p. 3.

traditional societies have a unique relationship with the land, which they view as capable of use only, not ownership. Some view the earth in its entirety as a living organism capable of injury and hurt.[238]

In many African countries, traditional rules and cultural belief systems reign. Respect for, and adherence to such traditional rules and cultural belief systems are expected from companies that operate in the locality where such beliefs permeate. These traditional rules expressed sometimes as "by-laws" have been transmitted orally from generations to generations and enforced by taboos, management in time and seasons, religious sanctions and sanctions through traditional authorities. Traditional rules/cultural belief systems may seek to for example protect a community's drinking water resource, forest, rivers or lagoons and their resources. However, very often the basis for protection is not founded on accurate science but on superstition. For example a river or its surrounding forest lands may be protected on the basis that the spirit of the river god resided in the forest.[239]

Such beliefs are enforced through taboos and such taboos would include : prohibition of cultivation of forest lands in the river banks, prohibition of use of fisheries resources within the river and restrictions on access to the river on certain days[240] as well as restriction of discharge of even treated effluent into the rivers and lagoons. These taboos thus serve to prevent the defilement of the river. Thus although protection of the forests along river banks was based on religious and cultural beliefs, it served as river corridor management. Increasingly it is being argued that aspects of such traditional concepts should be formally integrated into formal legal systems.[241]

[238] *Ibid*, p. 4.

[239] Ntiamoa-Baidu, Y. "Indigenous vs. Introduced Biodiversity Conservation Strategies: The case of protected areas systems in Ghana", (1995), African Biodiversity Series, Number I, May 1995, 1-11, Washington: The Biodiversity Support Program.

[240] Ntiamoa-Baidu, Y. "Conservation of coastal lagoons in Ghana: the traditional approach", (1991), Landscape and Urban Planning, Amsterdam: Elsevier Science Publishers B.V, Vol. 20, 41-46.

[241] *Ibid.*

Many indigenous people[242] see land as the home of the ancestors, the provider of everyday material needs, and the future held in trust for coming generations. According to the indigenous view, land should not be torn open and exploited- this is a violation of the Earth, neither oner be bought, sold or bartered. Furthermore, indigenous peoples have, over a long period of time, developed successful systems of land use and resource management. These systems, including nomadic pastoralism,[243] shifting cultivation,[244] various forms of agro-forestry,[245] terrace agriculture,[246] hunting, herding and fishing, were for a long time considered inefficient, unproductive and primitive. However, as world opinion grows more conscious of the environment and particularly of the damage being done to fragile habitats, there has been a corresponding interest in indigenous land-use practices. The notion of sustainability is the essence of both indigenous economies and their cultures.

[242] Considering the diversity of indigenous peoples, an official definition of "indigenous" has not been adopted by any United Nations-system body. Instead the system has developed a modern understanding of this term based on the following: -Self-identification as indigenous peoples at the individual level and accepted by the community as their member; Historical continuity with pre-colonial and/or pre-settler societies; Strong link to territories and surrounding natural resources; Distinct social-economic or political systems; Distinct language, culture and beliefs; Resolve to maintain and reproduce their ancestral environments and systems as distinctive peoples and communities.

[243] This is the grazing of cattle and sheep wherein the animals are moved within periods and in respect of seasons.

[244] Shifting cultivation is a form of land use among resource poor communities with a rotation of cultivation and fallow in the same unit of land. Millions of indigenous people are dependent on shifting cultivation practice, with majority households for subsistence living. This practice is in transition these days with rising population of shifting cultivators and demand for more food. GandhivKafle, An Overview of Shifting Cultivation with Reference to Nepal, (2011), International Journal of Biodiversity and Conservation Vol. 3(5), p. 147-154, available online http://www.academicjournals.org/ijbc, (lastly accessed 23/8/2018).

[245] In the most basic sense, agro-forestry means planting trees in agricultural or foraging areas. But in many parts of the world, agro-forestry is the traditional method of farming. However, traditional methods are being lost and forgotten due to the push toward high production and continuous planting made possible with chemical fertilizers and pesticides. But the land cannot sustain this kind of intense production. What makes this dangerous is that farmers will be unable to return to traditional methods or at least incorporate them because they no longer have the knowledge to do so. The right combinations of plants and timing are crucial to success. The various forms of agro-forestry include: Trees on farmland, Parkland also known as scattered trees, Alley cropping, Wind breakers and shelter belts. See Alao J. S. and Shuaibu, R. B., "Agroforestry Practices and Concepts in Sustainable Land use Systems in Nigeria", (2013), Journal of Horticulture and Forestry, Vol. 5(10), pp. 156-159.

[246] Terracing refers to building a mechanical structure of a channel and a bank or a single terrace wall, such as an earthen ridge or a stone wall. Terracing reduces slope steepness and divides the slope into short gently sloping sections. Terraces are created to intercept surface runoff, encourage it to infiltrate, evaporate or be diverted towards a predetermined and protected safe outlet at a controlled velocity to avoid soil erosion. See LuukDorren and Freddy Rey, "A review of the effect of terracing on erosion", Scape Soil Conservation and Protection for Europe, p. 97-108 at p. 97. available at www.scape.org , accessed on the 05/07/2016.

At the international level, ILO Convention No.169 on Indigenous Peoples[247] and Article 8 of the Convention on Biological Diversity[248] contain provisions protecting the traditional lifestyles and knowledge of indigenous peoples and local communities. National or local laws and policies may protect or may adversely affect marginalised and disadvantaged communities, especially indigenous or tribal communities following traditional lifestyles. In some instances, indigenous people have been forced from their traditional lands to make way for development projects (see Narmada case in India), or have found that resources have been exploited, including deforestation of their traditional lands.[249] Some indigenous people have seen their traditional lands declared protected areas where they are no longer permitted to live. Enforcing traditional laws and norms that guarantee or protect the land and resource rights of such communities has been an important means of ensuring environmental protection in some jurisdictions.

In Cameroon in particular, an important aspect of culture and belief that ensured environmental protection was the imposition of sacred sites in the villages. This created some sanctuary for wildlife species. These areas were totally protected, feared and revered by all. No one was allowed to move into such areas to hunt. In the Western Regions of Cameroon today, the only areas left where there is some semblance of intact forests are the sacred forests around palaces of traditional rulers.[250] No doubt Achoundong[251] and Dogmo[252] claimed that the Mbing Mekoup reserve would not still exist were it not for its sacred nature, which was highly valued and well protected by the Mondoni (Bamock) and the Bamileke of Bangang village in the Western Region (Province as it then was). Though they are empty forests, devoid of substantial wildlife, these are areas where one can still find indigenous species of trees.

---

[247] ILO Convention No.169 on Indigenous and Tribal Peoples, 1989.

[248] Article 8 (a-k) of the United Nations Convention on Biological Diversity 1992.

[249] Examples include the destruction of the forestry habitat of the Bakola, "Pygmy along the Chad – Cameroon Oil Pipeline, some kribi communities displaced by the construction of the Kribi Deep Sea Port.

[250] Kaba Eric Tah, "The African Conservation Delima: Ancient Tradition vs. Modern Greed, in Wildlife Justice, African Traditions and Wildlife Conservation", (2012), Bilingual Wildlife Law Enforcement Journal, N0 008, 1-12, p.3.

[251] Achoundong G, *Le Bois Sacre de la Chefferie Bafou*, (Herbier National, Yaoundé 1990), Mimeo, p. 7

[252] Chi Augustine, Co-management of Forest in Cameroon: The Compatibility of Government Policies with Indigenous Practices, (University of Twente,, Drienerveld, 1999), p.10.

On the same line of reasoning but for the North West Region, Chi Augustin[253] cites the example of the Bafut Kingdom sacred forests of the Bafut people in the North West Region, as he ascertains that religious beliefs and institutional constraints play an important role in the protection of the groves. Most crucial are myths that the forest is the abode of ancestors/gods.[254] This myth endows the area with an aura of sacredness. While the forests could be protected, the vegetation there protected, animals could never benefit from the same kind of protection as they would always stray away from the sacred area.

Cameroonian cultures were built around strong traditional institutions that would oversee and regulate the killing of animals and the purposes for which these animals were killed. The grassland regions in Cameroon do have strong and powerful "*Afon*"[255] and sacred societies – the "*Kwihfons*"[256], and the "*Ngumbas*"[257] whose word was law and order at the same time. These institutions have lost some of their authority to the modern institutions of the State and so some of these matters are treated by State institutions. The State institutions are finding it very difficult to play the role inherited from African

[253] *Ibid.*

[254] As a sacred forest that is venerated as the abode of the gods, the area cannot be entered freely and cultivated, or used to pick or fetch forest products (fuel wood). The myths prescribe certain frightening diseases (like madness) likely to befall whoever violates any of these stipulations. The threat of supernatural sanctions always take the form of an incapacitating illness leading to death, or death itself, if an offending person fails to subject himself to ritual cleansing. An example is the case of Mme Ako and Mr Amahbow who he said are mad, because they, without permission, entered the sanctuary to see the shrines.

[255] The appellation '*Fon*' has raised a lot of controversy. It has been difficult to trace the origin of this word given that the chieftaincy Decree of 1977 does not refer to Afon but to Chiefs. The Fon who is the head of the Fondom and though being part of the *Kwihfon* functions under it. He is installed by the *Kwihfon* and mandated by the people, with whom he deals on a daily basis. He ensures the functioning of indigenous traditional institutions and approves some.

[256] The *Kwihfon* as it is called in Oku and *Kwifon* in Bafut, are secret societies which serve as central and supreme institution in these communities. It is the indigenous law-maker, the interpreter and enforcer and the executor. The *Kwihfon* is the power-house of indigenous and traditional institutions in the communities where they exist. It is the 'owner' of all land in Oku, and this includes the forest and the people. Rooted in beliefs, the *Kwihfon* institution protects the forest essentially through its injunctions. See Tamasang, C. F, Community Forest Management Entities as Effective tool for Local Level Participation under Cameroonian Law: A Case Study of Kilum/Ijim Mountain Forest, (PhD Thesis, University of Yaoundé II, Soa 2008), (Unpublished), p. 119.

[257] The *Ngumba* just like the *Kwifon*, is a secret society of notables and law makers and one can only become a member through initiation in to it and it is the highest organ. It is a male regulatory society from which women are excluded. This society performs most of the local rituals and owns all of the land in the Fondom. Most of the notables belong to this society, as do traditional healers and soothsayers. This society has the power to judge and deliberate cases and its sentences must be respected.

cultures. Unlike the traditional conservation systems, were control was rooted deep inside the consciences of everyone and some of the fears of repercussions were so deep that no one dared go against any taboo, any law or regulation that was in place, control today is external and exercised by the government, through laws. This control has oneribe limitations and the destruction of wildlife species has continued. To safeguard these ancestral heritage that serve as habitat for others, there was absolute need for responsibilities to be imposed on major actors of environment-companies.

3.5 Conclusion

The notion of corporate social responsibility in environmental governance has emerged to provide a connection with the three pillars of sustainable development – economic, environmental and social. We learn that companies that respond effectively to the challenges of sustainability can gain a competitive advantage, exploit new market opportunities, boost market share, increase shareholder value, and become more profitable. The above experiences have proved that effective protection and proper governance of the environment requires commitments at the international and national levels as well as public and private participation. Indeed Chapter 30 of Agenda 21 of the Rio Conference 1992 highlighted the role of business in achieving sustainable development.

From this line of reasoning, since corporate institutions are said to constitute the threat, there was the urgent need to check their activities. Equally, there was the need for states to abide not only with fundamental human rights as established by the international community, but also to uphold and act in line with environmental law principles enshrined in international environmental treaties and conventions. Important also, was traditional and cultural belief systems, which was ascertained not only to have positively enhanced the protection of nature and natural resources but the fact that some protected areas even served as habitat for indigenous people. There was need therefore, for legal instruments to define and shape corporate responsibility viz a viz the environment. This indicates clearly why Cameroon has for long been grappling with the concept of corporate responsibility in environmental governance ; a concept that has transcended stages in the search for its right position and has become what it is today. Consequently, it is possible to identify within the context of available judicial authorities and legislative enactments. The big question that one may possibly be tempted to answer at this juncture is whether the concept is sufficiently articulated such that the specific responsibilities effectively guarantee environmental governance. This initiates the need to develop the concept, identify and analyse the specific environmental responsibilities in corporate social responsibility in a bid to ascertain its effectiveness in guaranteeing environmental governance. This is the focus of chapter four of this research.

CHAPTER FOUR

COMPLIANCE AND ENFORCEMENT MECHANISMS

4.0 Introduction

Cameroon is not free from the 'electricity and water curse'. The benefits that go with the exploitation of electricity, water and oil do not accrue to Cameroonians in the same way as Norwegians benefit from its oil exploitation. Local communities hosting hydro-electricity and water production facilities have nothing to show for this. For example, it has been indicated earlier that most of the areas hosting hydro-electrical equipments in Cameroon barely have a single kilometer of tarred road. The roads are near impassable during some seasons. Social amenities which permit people to lead dignified lives, are near absent or where they exist, they are in a rudimentary state. There is equally a steady environmental degradation. For example, Cameroonians living along the Chad-Cameroon pipeline project suffer the adverse environmental effects of the project.[258] Even at the terminal in Kribi, inhabitants have lost their means of livelihood as a result of the pipeline. Deep-water horizon drilling in the Gulf of Guinea is a potential danger to aquatic life and coastal inhabitants. This notwithstanding, some measure of legal control of the industry exists. The government and these utility services are engaged in a wide range of initiatives aimed at enhancing the quality of life and the quality of the environment. But Cameroon still remains a country with poor social indicators.

[258] The Washington based NGO – the Environmental Defence Fund (EDF), a fierce critic of the project predicted: "The 600 mile underground pipeline through Cameroon will pass through ecologically fragile rainforest areas . . . As a result, deforestation, wildlife poaching and the loss of farmland of the local villages to the construction activities will create a destructive environmental legacy. The pipeline itself even with state of the art technology, poses the danger of groundwater contamination and pollution of important regional water systems as crude oil containing heavy metals leaks into the environment" see http://www.edf.org/pubs/reports/c_chadcam.

This chapter argues that the problem lies in the monitoring and enforcement mechanism. Cameroon is a country with a weak and unreliable judiciary. What is more, the justiciability of economic and social rights are problematic.[259] The legislature is largely captured by the executive, rendering it incapable of performing its roles which consists of representing constituent interests, making or shaping public policy and overseeing policy implementation by executive branch agencies.[260]

The inability of the legislature to legislate appropriately and to oversee effectively, is at the root of the mismatch between electricity, water and oil industries activities and inability to enhance the human right to development and the right to a healthy environment. This mismatch is at the base of the disparity between normative expectations and observed outcomes. This chapter therefore examines the mechanism for the enforcement of existing laws affecting the hydro-electricity and water industries beginning with the question whether the environmental and human rights are justiciable, and also examines the roles of the judiciary and legislature in the oversight of the activities of the industries. Further the chapter considers the possibility of bringing actions against electricity and water companies in Cameroon.

4.1 Role of the Legislator

Cameroon's natural resources have for many decades been a source of power and wealth for the country's ruling elites and for multinational corporations, and less often for ordinary Cameroonians. Tragically and repeatedly, competition for control of revenues from natural resources has fueled cycles of corruption and poverty, forestalling opportunities to spur economic growth and social development. As global mineral and petroleum resources grow scarcer in other countries and on other continents, and new African

---

[259] Deval Desai, "COURTING" LEGITIMACY: DEMOCRATIC AGENCY AND THE JUSTICIABILITY OF ECONOMIC AND SOCIAL RIGHTS, Interdisciplinary Journal of HumanRights Law, 2009-2010

[260] Shari B, & Barrie H, Transparency and accountability in Africa's Extractive Industry: The Role of the Legislature, NDI, 2007.

sources come into production, resource-rich African nations like Cameroon are earning rising profits from their natural wealth. If these resources are to be used effectively and harnessed for development, more accountable and transparent mechanisms must be developed and supported by the government, multinational corporations, the legislature, political parties, civic organizations and the media. This section discusses the place of elected political officials – particularly those in the legislative branch of government – in serving as constructive leaders in improving the oversight and management of the country's oil resources so as to achieve economic development. Democratic governance requires legislatures to serve three purposes: representing citizen interests; making or shaping laws and policies; and overseeing the executive.[261] In the management and control of the activities of the electricity, water and oil industries, legislators bear responsibility for ensuring that policy and regulatory frameworks support their sustainable use and exploitation, and that government agencies appropriately allocate and account for revenues.[262] This section identifies the challenges that Cameroonian legislators face in overseeing the country's energy and water industries.

In Cameroon, while current efforts to increase transparency and accountability in the management of energy and water resources, emphasise the roles and responsibilities of a broad range of actors, relatively little attention has been paid to the potential contribution of elected legislators. Yet, the three core functions of the legislative body – representing constituent interests, making or shaping public policy, and overseeing policy implementation by executive branch agencies – are central to any effort in this area.

The recognition of the need to improve management of the utility industries in Cameroon presents a unique opening for legislators to establish themselves as relevant and credible actors in the movement towards greater transparency,

---

[261] *Ibid.*, at p 10

[262] The National Democratic Institute for International Affairs (NDI) believes that African legislatures could play more robust roles in creating viable oversight mechanisms to monitor the collection and use of revenues from extractive industry revenues, and in ensuring that the interests of civil society and citizens are taken into account, from community-level environmental concerns to the allocation and disbursement of revenues collected by central governments.

accountability and responsiveness in government. Initiatives like the Extractive Industries Transparency Initiative (EITI) and Publish What You Pay (PWYP) Coalition have drawn worldwide attention to the need for increased transparency and accountability in the management of extractive industries. The result is unprecedented international political will, information and tools for reforming management of the extractive industries.

Similarly, the window of opportunity for legislators to prove themselves as relevant and capable actors in the debate over extractive industry management closed firmly in a country like Cameroon where the legislature has limited credibility in the eyes of citizens.

The Cameroonian legislators face many constraints in fulfilling their roles and responsibilities, including weak individual and institutional capacity, little independence from the more powerful executive and ruling political party, and limited political will.[263] Oversight of the utility industries is further complicated by a common perception held by many legislators themselves that the industry's technical complexity is beyond their comprehension.[264] Faced with proposals from well-informed or connected executive branch agencies or officials, legislators often lack both the information and the confidence to influence legislation, policy or management of the utility industries.

A weak legislature cannot serve as a counterweight to a more powerful executive branch. In Cameroon, the concept of party loyalty is so strong that the legislature is marginalized from the decision-making process and dissuaded from conducting oversight activities. Ruling party control is pervasive, and the legislature is often used to rubber stamp executive policy after little or no debate. Constitutions, legislation and other rules of procedure often vest significant legal authority in the executive, thereby diminishing the ability of legislatures to oversee the oil sector.[265]

[263] Cf supra
[264] *Ibid.*
[265] *Ibid.*

In a large number of the countries surveyed by the National Democratic Institute for International Affairs,[266] legislators are sidelined by more powerful executives, and often lack the information and skills to fulfill their core functions. When the role of the legislative branch as a counterbalance to executive power is not fully developed, customary practice frequently gives the executive disproportionate power and authority.[267] The complex environment in which electricity and water exploitation frequently occurs makes it particularly difficult for legislators to exercise effective oversight. Cameroonian law does not grant the National Assembly the power to investigate state-owned companies. Legislators are often under pressure to pass budgets within time frames that do not allow for diligent review.

Regulation and oversight of the energy and water industries require an understanding of complex technical and financial issues. In Cameroon, the ability of individual legislators to understand and contribute to extractive sector management in general and oversight is worrisomely weak. The lack of formal education among certain legislators accounts for the lack of understanding. Equally, high turnover in the legislature makes it difficult for legislators to build up specific areas of expertise over time.

Ultimate responsibility for the management of a country's energy and water resources' wealth lies with that country's elected government. The principal means of ensuring sound management at all stages of electricity and water resources exploitation – from extraction to the collection and expenditure of revenues – is through the adoption of practices that adhere to and reinforce agreed upon standards of accountability and transparency. Countries that have successfully used proceeds from the extractive industries for national development purposes, including Australia, Canada and Norway, have such practices in common.[268]

---

[266] Shari, B & Barrie H. Transparency and Accountability in Africa's Extractive Industries, National Democratic Institute for International Affairs (NDI) 2007

[267] *Ibid.*

[268] *Ibid.*

According to a study commissioned by the World Bank,

> Our findings stress the importance of strong (or at least strengthened) institutions in the wake of natural resource discoveries as a way to curb the negative growth effects of corruption. This is especially true in less developed countries where natural resource discoveries have a much higher relative impact on both the capital stock and the extent of corruption, and are confronted with generally weaker and less adaptable institutions.[269]

Accountable governments face two principal challenges in determining the policy framework for the exploitation of oil and energy in their countries. First, they must create a business climate that attracts private investment, a necessary precondition to the development of the extractive industries. Second, they must address relevant domestic policy issues, such as the environmental impact on communities affected by extraction activities, and ensure the equitable distribution of profits from the industry. Policy or regulatory frameworks and laws governing the exploitation and management of natural resources are often spread across different pieces of legislation and other government instruments. In most cases, constitutions vest natural resources in the people but grant the government the authority to manage those resources on their behalf. In some cases, constitutions specify formulae for revenue sharing between national and state or provincial levels of government. Mining, environmental, electricity, water codes specify procedures and parameters for the granting of concessions and other rights of access, general conditions for exploitation, royalties, taxes, and other incentives specific to the extractive industries.

Corporate tax structures and laws governing employment, the environment, and occupational health and safety also have implications for extractive industry management. Through their lawmaking functions, legislators can support the passage of laws or other instruments that create an enabling

[269] Leite and Weidman, quoted in Marshall, Ian, *A Survey of Corruption Issues in the Mining & Mineral Sector*. England:International Institute for Environment and Development,2001. Availableonlineat:http://www.iied.org/mmsd/mmsd_pdfs/marshall_corruption.pdf

environment for sustainable and accountable management of oil, electricity and water. Recommendations made by the Norwegian Parliament helped determine the appropriate management systems when large offshore oil and gas deposits were discovered in the late 1960s. The Norwegian legislature continues to play a central role in overseeing management of the extractive industries. Regrettably, legislators from a number of African countries described situations in which they were under pressure to move legislation forward quickly, often without amendment, because funding from international development partners depended on the passage of legislation.[270] Confidentiality clauses are also often used to prevent public scrutiny of contract details.[271]

In the most successful economies, the state's role as facilitator of investment is balanced by its role, for example, as regulator – establishing laws and policies that provide for regional land use planning, ameliorate environment and social impacts, or take advantage of the opportunity to develop roads, schools, and better health care.[272]

The Cameroon legislator's inability to monitor and oversee the activities of the oil industry so as to guarantee the rights to development and a healthy environment, is clearly portrayed in the Chad Cameroon pipeline project.

The Cameroonian legislator has laid down corporate social responsibility for multinationals with the view to attaining the general objectives of the law. For preventive reasons, the law imposes mandatory requirements aimed at regulating corporate conduct in a bid to contain climate change. These responsibilities have been classified under two broad categories: preventive responsibilities and curative responsibilities.

[270] See note 2 supra

[271] Cf supra note 3, p 11

[272] The Mining, Minerals and Sustainable Development Project. *Breaking New Ground: Mining Minerals and Sustainable Development.* London: Earthscan Publications Ltd, 2002. Report for the International Institute for Environment and Development and the World Business Council for Sustainable Development.

For preventive reasons, the law imposes mandatory requirements aimed at regulating corporate conduct in a bid to contain climate change. These responsibilities have been classified under two broad categories: preventive responsibilities and curative responsibilities.

4.1.1 Preventive Responsibilities

Since it is arguably cost effective to prevent environmental harm than repairing harm done to the environment, decisions and policies most often align with the saying that prevention is better than cure. In line with this, preventive responsibilities have been outlined for corporate bodies with the aim of adverting social and environmental harm. These responsibilities include: Environmental Impact Assessment, Corporate Environmental Disclosure or Reporting, Environmental Auditing and Monitoring.

4.1.1.1 Environmental Impact Assessment (EIA)

This is the first and most evident responsibility of a preventive character which has been articulated in most legal instruments having a bearing on CSR both international and national. Environmental Impact Assessment[273] has been a central component of these statutes and this was made a mandatory process for most large-scale developments. Citing Sadler[274], Bitondo[275] defines Environmental Impact Assessment as a process of collecting, organising, analysing, interpreting and communicating information that is relevant to the consideration for each particular application. EIA has equally been defined as "*the formal and systemic collection and analysis of information relating to the possible environmental effects of new or significantly altered projects in relation to the physical, social and economic environment surrounding that*

[273] Herein after referred to as EIA.

[274] Sadler B. (1996), *Environmental Assessment in a Changing World: Evaluating Practice to Improve Performance*. International Study of the Effectiveness of Environmental Assessment.Final Report. Canadian Environmental Assessment Agency, International Association for Impact Assessment, UNCED (1992) & Agenda 21.https://www.ceaa.gc.ca/Content/2/B/7/2B7834CA-7D9A-410B-A4ED-FF78AB625BDB/iaia8_e.pd.

[275] Bitondo D., "Environmental Assessment in Cameroon: State of the Art", (2000), *Impact Assessment and Project Appraisal*, 18 (1), pp. 33-42, available at http://dx.doi.org/10.3152/147154600781767592. p. 34, (last visited 15/06/2019).

development".[276] The Prime Ministerial Decree on its part defines EIA as: "*a systematic examination in view of determining whether or not a project has an unfavourable effect on the environment*".[277]

EIA was introduced fully into the local law through Law No. 96/12 of 5 August 1996 relating to environmental management which was the first national legislation on environmental management. Section 17 of this law provides as follows:

(1) The promoter or owner of any development, project, labour or equipment, which is likely to endanger the environment, owing to its dimension, nature or the impact of its activities on the natural environment shall carry out an environmental impact assessment. This assessment shall determine the direct or indirect incidence of the said project on the ecological balance of the zone where the plant is located or any other region, the physical environment and quality of life of populations and the impact on the environment in general.

(2) The environment impact assessment shall be included in the file submitted for public investigation where such a procedure is provided for.

(3) The impact assessment shall be carried out at the expense of the promoter.

The 1996 Framework Law on Environmental Management in Cameroon[278] emphasises on EIA. EIA is prescribed in Section 16 of this law.[279] Being the main legislation on environmental management, Section 17 of the Law prescribes EIA for all projects, which have a propensity to degrade the environment.[280] The multiple definitions notwithstanding, one thing that stands out clear is that the essence of EIA is to ascertain the effect of a project on the environment prior to its execution.

---

[276] Article 2 of the 1992 United Nations Convention on Biological Diversity.

[277] Article 2 of Decree No.96/0577/PM of February 2005 Fixing the Modalities for the Realisation of Environmental Impact Assessment in Cameroon (hereinafter referred to as the decree).

[278] Law No. 96/12 of 5th August 1996 relating to Environmental Management in Cameroon (hereinafter referred to as the Environmental Code).

[279] *Ibid*, Section 16.

[280] See Section 17, *ibid*.

Later on, Decree No. 2013/0171/PM to lay down rules for conducting environmental and social impact assessment (hereinafter referred to as the 2013 Decree) will amend and replace Decree No. 2005/0577. The 2013 decree explicitly mentions the social aspect of the impact study, as it is refers to environmental and social impact assessment (ESIA) rather than to environmental impacts assessment (EIA). This caused a change in appellation from EIA to ESIA. This appellation has officially been recognised and became a peculiarity of Cameroon. The 2013 decree also introduced strategic environmental and social assessment (SEA) and the environmental impact statement (EIS) as tools for environmental assessment.

The latest improvement on ESIA was carried out in February 2016 with two Ministerial Orders; one to elaborate on the categories of operations subject to ESIA and SEA, and the other to define the content for a modelled terms of reference (ToR).

In fulfilment of the stipulations of Article 6 of the Prime Ministerial Decree,[281] Ministerial Orders No. 0069/MINEP (Arrête No. 0069/MINEP) and Ministerial Order No. 0070/MINEP (Arrêté No.0070/MINEP) were established in March 2005 and 22 April 2005, respectively by the Minister of Environment and Nature Protection (MINEP). These Ministerial Orders prescribe the different categories of projects that would require an EIA. Order No.0070/MINEP fixed the different categories of projects submitted to Environmental Impact Assessment. The uniqueness and importance of this text is drawn from the fact that it clearly spells out the details of projects that must be submitted to either simple EIA or detailed EIA.[282] The difference between the two types of impact assessment is evident not only in the type of project to be executed, but also, the content of the impact assessment report. Article 4 of the Prime Ministerial Decree[283] elaborates the elements that must

[281] Article 6 (1) provides that "*the list of projects (activities) that must be submitted of either categories of Environmental Impact Assessment referred to in Articles 4 and 5 above shall be fixed by the Minister in charge of the Environment*". It should be noted that the categories referred to here is the Summary and Detailed environmental Impact Assessment.

[282] Summary impact assessment and detailed impact assessment. See Article 2(1) Order No.0070/MINEP fixed the different categories of projects submitted to Environmental Impact Assessment.

[283] Decree No. 2005/0577/PM of February 2005 Enacting the Process and Procedural Framework Governing EIA in Cameroon.

be found in the content of the environmental Impact report.[284] These laws classify projects requiring an EIA into two categories.[285]

Order No. 0070/MINEP of 22 April 2005 has provided a list of activities that must be submitted to simple or detailed impact assessment. This means that not all activities or projects are required to undergo EIA before execution. The Order fails to advance any justification why only the identified list of projects must be submitted to EIA. Furthermore, it is worth stating that the Order, in listing the activities whose execution must be preceded by EIA, does not highlight any particular reason why it is a simple or detailed impact assessment that is required for the particular activity.

From the foregoing, it becomes clear that the current legislation for EIA in Cameroon is the Framework Law on Environmental Management, the application of which is enabled by Decree No. 2013/0171/PM. These legislations provide for three types of EIA that must be conducted under Cameroonian law by the promoter or owner of any development, project, labour or equipment, which is likely to endanger the environment, owing to its dimension, nature or the impact of its activities on the natural environment. These include ESIA, the SEA and the EIS. This is in conformity with the trend in international legal practice which has evolved to lay emphasis on the social aspect of the impact study and also the development of strategic environmental impact assessment. In fact, Article 7 of the 2013 Decree provides that the promoter or owner of any development project, establishment, programme or policy, must carry out an ESIA, SEA or EIS under pain of sanctions envisaged in the law inforce. The 2013 Decree also provides that the list of activities subject to ESIA and SEA and the content of the ToR will be provided by an Order of the minister in charge of environment[286] while the list of activities subject to EIS shall be provided by

[284] A description of the environment of the site and the region; Description of the project; A report of field work; An inventory and the description of the impacts of the project on the environment including envisaged mitigating measures together with an estimate of the corresponding cost; Approved terms of reference of the study; and Bibliographic references.

[285] Category one projects are those projects requiring a simple EIA while Category 2 projects are those projects requiring a detailed EIA study.

[286] Section 8 (1).

local councils in consultation with the decentralised services of the ministry in charge of the environment.[287]

Arguably, an element that might have been considered during the classification of the projects is the level of adverse effects the particular project is capable of generating on the environment and the community where it is supposed to be executed.

From the provisions of Section 11(1) and (2), effective public participation is a fundamental component of the EIA process.[288] This is because public participation increases the accountability and transparency of the decision-making process. However, looking at the current legal and procedural disposition regulating EIA in Cameroon, it is glaring that public participation is not statutorily protected. What impedes effective public participation is effective and efficient communication. During public consultation, available information to enable the public to participate effectively during public meetings is not easily grasped by the lay person. The problem is accentuated by the lack of public knowledge on legal issues and the fact that most legal documents in Cameroon exist only in one of the two languages.

The role and importance of public participation in environmental decision-making cannot be overlooked.[289] The European Commission further established that effective public participation in the taking of decisions enables the public to express their views, and the decision maker has to take account of options and concerns which may be relevant to those decisions, thereby increasing the accountability and transparency of the decision-making process and contributing to public awareness of environmental issues and support for the decisions taken. However, looking at the current legal and procedural disposition regulating EIA in Cameroon, it is glaring that public

[287] Section 8 (2).

[288] See Section 11(1) and (2) of the Prime Ministerial Decree.

[289] Tamasang, Christopher, 2008, '*Environmental Impact Assessment under Cameeroonian Law*' *in Environmental Law and policy in Cameroon –Towards making Africa the tree of life*, available at http://www.nomos-elibrary.de.agb. Accessed 13 April 2020.

participation is not statutorily protected. Indeed, it is poorly represented in terms of timing and communicational hurdles. In addition, it is regrettable to note most local companies and MNC's kin Cameroon do not in practice respect EIA.

The problem is even compounded by the fact that local communities are not fully integrated into this EIA procedure disregard of their observations, the latter can bring an action in an administrative court against the administration in charge of the environment and join the promoter of the project as a codefender. This can also be done on behalf of the communities by a civil society organisation and recognised under existing laws (associations, non-governmental organisations) working in the field of environmental protection. This then justifies not only their locus standi but also public interest in the prejudice that has been caused on the environment by violating the EMP. This can result in the suspension/withdrawal of the CEC by the administration in charge of the environment by a decision of the court without prejudice to criminal/civil sanctions.

Another basis for local community action is the principle of participation through which locus standi is extended to local communities that can bring an action on a public as a whole interest basis or through representatives in the interest of the community at large as per Article 8 (2) of the Law of Environmental Management. Such an action can be brought against the promoter who is acting in irregularity. Civil society organisations may also act as plaintiff on behalf of the local communities against violators of EIA regulations.

Corruption seems to have taken over this procedure which is a canker-worm that has eaten deep into the fabrics of the Cameroonian society affecting every area and sector, not leaving out EIA enforcement institutions. Corruption in the form of bribes, preferential treatment, nepotism, cronyism and even state capture can be observed in every stage of the law enforcement process in Cameroon.

4.1.1.2 Corporate Disclosure

Another responsibility of companies is the duty to disclose, otherwise known as corporate reporting. The concept of corporate environmental reporting has been defined as the process through which "*companies often disclose environmental information to their stakeholders to provide evidence that they are accountable for their activities and the resultant impact on the environment*".[290] It is equally understood as the process by which a corporation communicates information regarding the range of its environmental activities to a variety of stakeholders including employees, local communities, shareholders, customers, government and environmental groups. Corporate reporting is a recent social responsibility of a preventive nature which can be said to be demonstrated in any of the following three categories, namely: involuntary disclosure[291], mandatory disclosure[292] and voluntary disclosure[293].

Cameroon's CSR legal instruments do not expressly mention corporate reporting; neither do they provide a definition of the concept. One can only therefore, infer from the provision of the Environmental Code on the right of citizens to environmental information that corporations have a duty to report. Section 7 stipulates "*All persons shall have the right to be informed on the negative effects of harmful activities on man, health, and the environment, as well as on the measures taken to prevent or compensate for these effects*".[294] It may not be wrong to conclude that companies in Cameroon have a duty to disclose considering that they play a key role in climate change. To effectively enforce the right to environmental information, it is therefore logical for corporate institutions, whose activities impact the environment, to report on regular bases their environmental activities, the effects of such activities and the

---

290 Lodhia S., "Legitimacy Motives for World Wide Web (www) Environmental Reporting: An Exploratory Study into Present Practices in the Australian Minerals Industry", (2005), *Journal of Accounting and Finance*, 4, p. 1-15.

291 Involuntary disclosure is the disclosure of information about a company's environmental activities without its permission and against its will. Examples of involuntary disclosures are environmental campaigns, press and media exposes and court investigations.

292 Mandatory disclosure, on the other hand, is the disclosure of information about a company's environmental activities that is required by law.

293 Voluntary disclosure is the disclosure of information on a voluntary basis.

294 See Section 7(1) of the Environmental Code.

measures taken to mitigate and compensate any harm. In Cameroon, the most noticeable categories of disclosure are mandatory and voluntary disclosures.

Furthermore, the OHADA Uniform Act Relating to Commercial Companies and Economic Interest Groups stipulates "*All listed companies and, in certain circumstances, their unlisted subsidiaries, must publish their accounting and financial statements in a legal journal*".[295] The Uniform Act on OHADA Accounting Law on its part requires that all Public Limited Companies incorporated in any of the Member States of the OHADA, publish their financial statement.

The importance of the annual financial statement, among other things, is that it discloses to the stakeholders the financial health of the company and most importantly the social and environmental commitment of the company. This is because financial statements provide detail information on the social and environmental activities engaged by the company and the cost incurred in their execution. It is worth stating that not all financial statements have social and environmental aspects of the company incorporated within. In certain circumstances, or for some companies, the social and environmental activities and expenditures are reported in a separate document while for others it is contained in the Director's Report.

In certain sectors in Cameroon, especially chemical industry, the petroleum and gas sectors, the mining sector and other heavy polluting areas, the responsibility to report is even stated in the license granting authorisation to operate. This is rooted in the fact that Cameroon is a signatory to the United Nations Framework Convention on Climate Change (UNFCCC) and its implementation document, the Kyoto Protocol to the UNFCCC. Many companies have established reporting practices using Green House Gas (GHG) Accounting Methodologies such as the ISO 14064-1.[296] Unfortunately,

[295] See Articles 846-853 of the Uniform Act Relating to Commercial Companies and Economic Interest Groups

[296] See Companies Act 2006 (Strategic Report and Directors' Reports) Regulations 2013, paragraph 19. It is worthy to note that Cameroon is a signatory to the ISO which by implication means that the ISO standards should be applicable in Cameroon.

just like Environmental Impact Assessment, effective corporate social and environmental reporting in Cameroon is hindered by a number of challenges which can be summarised in three words: Continuity[297], Comparability[298] and Credibility.[299]

4.1.1.3 Environmental Auditing and Monitoring

Another very important practice companies must uphold if they must effectively observe their social and environmental requirements is environmental auditing and monitoring. Usually, environmental auditing and monitoring is most often incorporated in Environmental Management Systems,[300] which are procedural rules for the organisation that assist managers in preventing and detecting environmental violations. They assist managers to comply with existing legal requirements and to define management processes to be followed in order to control the impact of a corporation's activities on the environment.[301]

Environmental monitoring involves the on-going checking, inspection, examination of equipment, management system, operational activities and their effects on the environment on a regular and frequent basis.[302] Monitoring is exercised at different levels and involves different categories. The different types of monitoring involve monitoring equipment to ensure they are in good working order, the company's impact on the environment,[303] the state of the

---

[297] Continuity can be ensured by publishing environmental reports with regular intervals, by setting targets and reporting back on progress and by using the same performance indicators over time.

[298] Comparability, on the other hand, is best achieved by using standardised and normalised environmental performance indicators. Mandatory disclosure in the Annual Report and Financial Statements will also improve the comparability.

[299] Credibility will only be achieved by openness and balanced tone in the report. Engaging stakeholders in dialogue is an important part of the process. Verification of environmental reports will only add credibility when the value of the verification statement is clear and the credibility of the verifier is higher than the credibility of the company itself.

[300] Hereinafter referred to as EMS.

[301] Babalola Olabisi A.., 'Seminar paper on Energy and Natural Resource Law', (Faculty of Law, University of Lagos, June 3-4, 2006), p. 34.

[302] Kimerling J. (1994) "Environmental Justice or Business as Usual?The Case of Environmental Monitoring and Audit of Texaco's Amazon Oil fields", 7 *Harvard Human Rights Journal*, pp. 199 - 200.

[303] For example emission levels, waste and the amount of energy used.

environment,[304] the implementation of environmental impact studies and the management processes. Monitoring ensures compliance with environmental and social regulations and with any conditions imposed on development on the basis of Environmental and Social Impact Assessment (ESIA).[305] It provides a tool for the company to evaluate and update mitigation strategies. By observation in Cameroon, such measures are not effective enough which result at times to poor environmental degradation caused by the activities of these local companies and MNCs.

Environmental auditing on its part is the practice of comparing environmental regulatory and management requirements against the operational and management performance record of a facility by evaluating such records and systems against a set of predetermined standards.[306] It is a systematic, periodical evaluation of a company's environmental performance and systems against pre-determined standards. The International Organisation for Standardisation (IOS) has developed standards for environmental auditing.[307] These standards are focused on audits of environmental management systems, rather than on compliance with legal regulations. The ISO Standards are considered to be the largest and most influential efforts towards standardising environmental auditing. This serves as a guide for companies to conduct self-audit, using the established standards to ascertain their level of compliance with the predetermined standard.

4.1.2 Curative Responsibility

Unlike preventive responsibilities, the Cameroonian legislator is informed that irrespective of all the efforts put in place to check corporate conduct through CSR, circumstances would arise where responsibilities would be violated and

---

[304] This involves the level of toxicity of water courses affected by resource exploitation and corporate pollution.

[305] This is in line with Sections and 9 of the 2011 Electricity Law.

[306] Kimerling J., *loc. Cit.*, note 62, p. 200 - 201.

[307] These are ISO 14010, 1996 Guidelines for Environmental Auditing, General Principles, ISO 14011, 1996, Guidelines for Environmental Auditing, Auditing Producers, Auditing of EMS, and ISO 14010: 1996 Guide lines for Environmental Auditing Qualification criteria for Environmental Auditors.

social and environmental harm perpetrated. This is true as certain projects cannot be executed without a resultant negative social and environmental impact. Also, the line of business for some companies is naturally socially and environmentally unfriendly. With these scenarios in mind, in order to ensure that damages resulting from such situations are effectively managed to minimise their impacts on the environment and the community at large, a curative responsibility has equally been articulated in the available legal instruments. Key within the framework of curative responsibility is the responsibility to mitigate environmental harm resulting from corporate activities.

4.1.2.1 Responsibility to Mitigate Environmental Harm

The duty on multinational corporations to mitigate environmental harm resulting from their operational activities is backed by the Polluter and User Pays Principle.[308] This principle equally integrates ENEO's environmental protection and economic activities by ensuring that the full environmental and social costs, including cost associated with pollution, resource degradation and environmental harm, are reflected in the ultimate market price for a good or service. This principle has been transcribed into the framework law on the protection of the environment in Cameroon.[309] This principle thus obliges corporate bodies to take the responsibility to mitigate such environmental harm resulting from their activities.

To begin with specific case scenarios, it is provided Section 9 of the 2011 Electricity Law that "... *the electricity operators that have been granted concessions and holders of licences duly established in accordance with the provisions of this law, shall have right of way to public roads and on portions of collective estates and settlements areas as well on surface and underground parts of non-built-estates, save otherwise provided by the laws and regulations in force.*

[308] Under this principle, states are enjoined to take actions necessary to ensure that polluters and users of natural resources bear the full environmental and social costs of their activities.

[309] Cf. Section 9 of the Cameroon Environmental Code. This law is to the effect that within the framework of regulations in force, rational environmental and natural resource management are based on principles. Amongst these, is the pollute and pay principle enshrined in Section 9, paragraph (c) of the Cameroon Environmental Code.

A cursory reading of the above disposition could simply be interpretated to explain the fact that in the event of damages to or accidents in any ship, aircraft, device or platform transporting or carrying hydro-electricity plants or harmful or dangerous electrical appliances in waters under Cameroonian jurisdiction, which may create a serious or imminent danger for the marine environment and its resources, the owner of the said electricity point shall be charged to pay for the rehabilitation of the damaged or contaminated site by the competent energy authorities, in application of the regulations in force.[310]

Confusing, however, is the fact that the legislator has neither stated any precise amount to be charged for the mitigation of the harm or rehabilitation of the site damaged by the corporate body nor even indicated that the amount shall be fixed by another law. It is our submission that this silence is tied to the reasoning that the intensity of the damage done and the degree of rehabilitation to be conducted can only be assessed on a per-occurrence basis. Section 9 of the Electricity law rather lays the financial burder on the electricity operator for the cost of oneribes environmental impact on activities that require an authorisation, concession or licence. Surprisingly, the occurrence of any environmental consequences resulting from these activities seems not to be the worry of the legislator in this text. Surprisingly, Section 9 rather, mandates the Minister of Water and Energy Resources to take precausionary measures in order to safeguard the continuance of public service, after the prior opinion of the Board. Section 97 (1) (b) and (C) rather provide withdrawal of the concession, licence, authorisation, and suspension of right to operate for a defaulter of the existing regulations in place. By a logical reasoning, such a measure seems to undermine the environmental rights of the local communities in some way because of the delay of justice which will be expected to emanate from the authorities in place.

In the same vein, but yet another instance, Section 91 of the 2011 Law provides that "*In all cases, the expenses and compensation costs accruing to any public or private interest and arising from the application of the provisions of Section 9 and 90 above shall be borne by the oneribesne or*

[310] This is also in line with Section 32 (1) of the Cameroon Environmental Code.

licensee."[311] In this line of activity, the practice seems to be that payment is an evaluation of the sum total of the expenses incurred by the authorities in the process of rehabilitating the site damaged.[312]

The position of this law is supported by other sector based laws on issues related to environmental protection of people as stipulated in Section 10 of the 2011 Law.[313] Interestingly, the Mining Code of Cameroon gives latitude for holders of mining permits and quarrying permits to choose to pay the financial cost of rehabilitation carried out by the competent administration.[314] In yet another circumstance, this time in the area of waste management, the duty to mitigate environmental harm resulting from corporate activities resurfaces. Section 48 stipulates: "*when wastes is abandoned, dumped or processed in violation of the prescriptions of this law, and its enabling regulations, the authority vested in police powers shall automatically eliminate the said waste at the expense of the said producer, after charging the producer to pay*."[315] Finally, the duty to mitigate environment harm can be interpreted in the obligation to rehabilitate exploitation sites. Typical of this is the provision of Section 61 of the Petroleum Code. This section is to the effect that "*the holder of authorisation or a petroleum contract shall repair any damages caused by its petroleum operations to the land used; it shall be liable in such case to pay a compensation amount commensurate to the damage caused, to be determined by mutual agreement between the parties concerned or, in default by the competent court*".Support to this is leant by Section 78, according to which rehabilitation work on the perimeter of the contract site should be done in accordance with the standards and practices in the international petroleum industry.[316] The purpose for this is to prevent damage of human life, property and the environment.

[311] Section 37 (1) of the Cameroon Environmental Code.

[312] See Section 48 (2) of the Cameroon Environmental Code which provides that: "*The administration shall oblige the producer to deposit to a public accountant a sum corresponding to the cost of the work done. The competent public accountant shall be appointed by order of the minister in charge of finance*".

[313] See Section 11 (3) of Law No. 1 of 16 April 2001, laying down the Mining Code. This section stipulates: "*Before an individual or corporate body is allowed to carry out mining operations, they must obtain a permit which shall be granted by a decree of the President of the Republic on the recommendation of the Minister in charge of Mines*".

[314] Section 37 (2), *ibid.*

[315] See Section 48 (1), *ibid.*

[316] Section 78 of the Petroleum Code.

CHAPTER FIVE

SANCTIONS FOR VIOLATION OF CORPORATE ENVIRONMENTAL RESPONSIBILITY

5.0 Introduction

Corporate social responsibility liability is a term used to describe the process through which the financial responsibility for environmental damage resulting from violation of CSR is transferred back to those who cause the damage. A well-designed CSR liability regime is also a significant deterrent to non-compliance with regulatory requirements. For CSR to be effective there must be a broad array of sanctions effectively enforced to deter certain conducts that do not concur with required standards. Determining appropriate punishment for misconduct is a difficult but vital task. The two regimes of civil law and criminal law both establish liability and sanctions for CSR offences.[317] The Cameroonian Environmental Code provides a series of sanctions that may be applicable to multinational corporations that commit either of the offences listed in the Code. Sanctions for violation of CSR have been grouped into two; extra judicial sanctions and judicial sanctions.

[317] Lipman Z. and Roots L. "Protecting the Environment through Criminal Sanctions: The Environmental Offences and Penalties Act 1989 (NSW)" (1995) 12 *Environment and Planning Law Journal*, pp. 16–36. Civil fines are essentially financial penalties which lack the moral overtones of comparable criminal sentences.

5.1 Extra Judicial Sanctions

A large number of corporate institutions have been sanctioned for violation of CSR. This indicates that significant progress has been recorded in the implementation of corporate social responsibility in Cameroon. Theoretically, the legislator supports this as provided in section 91.[318] Extra judicial or civil and administrative sanction refers to out of court measures taken by administrative authorities to bring to book CSR violators. These penalties range from fines, through confiscation, suspension and withdrawal of authorisation, order for rehabilitation, to order to stop a particular act.

5.1.1 Administrative Fines

The levying of fines on CSR offenders is the most frequently used sanction by the administration in Cameroon. These administrative fines are financial compensation for damage caused. The amount of fine imposed on the offender is determined by the gravity of the offence committed. Even when compounding is resorted to, the end result is usually the payment of a fine, the amount of which, as provided by the law, must not be less than the lower limit of the fine provided by the law against such offence. It should however be noted that the amount imposed as fine must not necessarily be the final amount paid. It depends on the final negotiations between the administration and the offender. By implication the State has the prerogative to assess such a payment in the occurrence of an offence. The State prefers the use of administrative sanctions to punish violators of CSR. The most frequently used of the variety of administrative sanctions is a fine. The imposition of fines by the administration on the violators of CSR is done after a breach has been ascertained.

[318] Section 91(1) of the Environmental Code. This Section is to the effect that "*The administrative units in charge of environmental management shall have the full right to effect a compromise. To do this, they shall be duly notified by the defaulter.*

Under the 2011 Electricity Law, fines have been levied in the case where the electricity operator's equipment or installation appliances do not comply with the prescribed standardisation norms.[319]

Also, where the electricity operator is found guilt of non-disclosing of any contractual information, Section 97 (2) (d) of the 2011 Law, places a levy ranging between 1,000 000 FCFA 5,000,000FCFA to be paid by the default electricity operator.

Going by the punishment outlined in Section 97, there is the temptation to laud the Ministry of Water and Energy Resources for inflicting this penalty in the form of fines.[320] Convincing as it may seem, though this Section was applied, it is far from satisfactory that a fine of 1,00,000 FCFA, 5,000,000FCFA, 4,000,000FCFA or 2,500,000FCFA should be deterrent to a big company like ENEO with exclusive exploitation of energy in Cameroon. Such measures should be tightened up with those available under the Environmental Law. Moreover, a similar decision was applied in the matter between ALUCAM Co Ltd v. MINEF.[321] In this case, ALUCAM was asked to pay a fine of 7,000,000FCFA which it did with little stress because the amount of money was too small for a big company like ALUCAM.[322] This further buttresses the argument that sanctions for violation of CSR in Cameroon are not sufficient deterrent to violators. Another argument in support of this fact is the uncountable environmental and financial damage caused by the incessant interruption of power failure to the consumers and operators in the agricultural, mining and petroleum sectors, just to mention a few.[323] The justification given for this by officials of MINEE is that the ENEO Company in Cameroon is still alone without any competitor in this sector.

---

[319] Section 97 (2) (c), Electricity Law.

[320] Section 79 of the Environmental Code.

[321] Matter No. 10/PVA/MINEF/BP/EF/SPE of 21 March 2001(unreported).

[322] ALUCAM was accused of discharging untreated industrial waste in River Sanaga and causing thermal pollution.

[323] It was recorded that a high suspicion of their outdated equipments and appliances which do not comply with the standardisation norms and eventually with the huge demands of consumers particularly in the rural areas seem to be the main cause of the problem.

An attempt at imposing draconian punishment on them will only force them to shut down and the possibility of attracting another operator might delay with time as the government faced with the oneri economic crisis seems to be financial ill-health to take back its economic sovereignty in this sector. With this kind of sanctions, the companies violate CSR because they can comfortably pay the fine.

Another issue that is disturbing is the discrimination in the penalty. This is because there is no fixed fine for the violation of CSR. Companies that violate CSR are indiscriminately fined. This discrimination is unhealthy, for it creates an atmosphere of uncertainty. This might hinder the punishment from achieving its deterrent objective. A high penalty will achieve this aim since no company will like to lose a huge amount of money because of failure to conduct environmental impact assessment and cause pollution of the air, which can be checked.

The disturbing issue here is why a company should be asked to pay damages when the exploitation of hydroelectricity is not possible to without damaging the environment by using its right of way on public roads, portion of collective estates, settlement areas, surface and underground parts of non-built-estates.[324] The reason for such EIA is to evaluate the effect the functioning of the company on the environment. If the effect outweighs the benefits then it will be improper to allow it function. This question however, becomes purposeful when the company conducts environmental impact assessment before carrying out its mining activities. However, authorisation to exploit natural resources such as electricity does not mean licence to destroy the environment.

The quantum of cases on the use of fines by the administration concerned to punish violators of CSR reveals that fines are much preferable to judicial

---

[324] Section 9, Electricity Law.

sanctions. As stated earlier, it is only when the offenders fail to comply with the ministerial sanction of a fine that such cases are referred to the court as the last resort. The question that warrants attention is whether the frequent use of fines implies its effectiveness as sanction for defaulters? The answer to this question is not in the affirmative. The frequent use of fines has demonstrated that a fine is not a sufficient disincentive to violation of CSR. This is evident in the number of companies that continuously breach the CSR and comfortably pay the fine imposed on them.

5.1.2 Suspension and Withdrawal of Exploitation Authorisation

Suspension is a temporal stop on the exploitation rights of a licence holder, when an alleged illegal act is said to have been committed or in cases of irregularities. Withdrawal on the other hand, is a complete termination or stop on the exploitation rights of a license holder because of the illegal act before the expiry of the duration of the license. The Environmental Code does not expressly encapsulate the right of the administration to suspend or withdraw licenses. Section 11 (3) of the 2011 Electricity Law however, recognises the right of the Minister of Water and Energy Resources to issue concessions or licences to qualified electricity bodies. Equally, the Environmental Law in its Section 38(1) however, recognises the right of the administration to issue exploitation authorisation or license to qualified bodies and individuals.[325] The position of this law is supported by other sector based laws.[326]

With regard to the electricity sector in Cameroon, owing to the fact that exploitation and trade licenses are issued by the administration, it is logical that

[325] Section 38(1) of the Environmental Code provides that "*The allotment and management of land for agriculture, industrial, urban or other uses, as well as prospecting, research or exploitation of subsoil resources likely to endanger the environment, shall be to the prior authorisation of each administration concerned and after the obligatory opinion of the administration in charge of the environment*".

[326] See Section 11 (3) of Law No. 1 of 16 April 2001, laying down the Mining Code. This section stipulates: "*Before an individual or corporate body is allowed to carry out mining operations, they must obtain a permit which shall be granted by a decree of the President of the Republic on the recommendation of the Minister in charge of Mines*".

the powers to suspend or withdraw such authorisations, in cases of violation, rest with the one who granted them and in this case it is the competent administration. Section 97 (1) (b) and (C) rather provide withdrawal of the concession, licence, authorisation, and suspension of right to operate for a defaulter of the existing regulations in place.

The power to pronounce such a decision is vested on the Minister in charge of Water and Energy Resources through the opinion of the Electricity Sector Regulatory Board (ARSEL). Legal backup to this is provided by the Framework Law on Environmental Management in Cameroon.[327]

It is required that for any suspension taken, the reasons should be stated and the offender notified. Unfortunately, it is difficult to lay hands on any cases of suspension or withdrawal of exploitation licenses by the administration in charge of environment. Usually where the administration chooses to suspend the license, the wrong doer would be required to pay a fine and stop the wrongful act. This only goes to confirm that a fine is the most preferred penalty used to punish CSR defaulters by the administration. If the Ministry is reluctant to drag violating companies to court, then it is even more reluctant to suspend or withdraw authorisations, licenses and concessions in order not to lose the economic benefits brought by these companies. The justification has always been the desire not to chase away the companies and to avoid the companies from closing down because of hard sanctions.

---

[327] Section 23(1) of this law provides that: "*when persons responsible for discharging pollutants into the atmosphere beyond the norms laid down by the administration do not respect regulations, the competent administration shall issue them a notice to pay in this light*". *Most importantly is the provision of sub-section 2 which states inter alia* that: "Where the notice to pay is ineffective or does not produce the estimated effects either within the prescribed deadline or automatically in an emergency, the competent administration shall, in consultation with the administration in charge of the environment and the others concerned suspend the functioning of the said plant or implement.........".See Section 23(2).

5.1.3 Conciliation and Arbitration

Arbitration has been held to be the most common ADR mechanism.[328] It is a formal measure where parties to an environmental dispute may settle their differences through a joint agreement before an arbitrator, in this case not usually named in advance because of the nature of the dispute. This is a provision of the framework law.[329] One may equally highlight the fact although the parties to the dispute have chosen arbitration, the outcome of it may not prejudiced a subsequent court action at the initiative of either of the parties intended to challenge the arbitral award, the competence of the arbitrator.

Conciliation and arbitration are alternative settlement mechanisms put in place by the Electricity Law and Water Law[330] in Cameroon. With conciliation, it brings together on the one hand ; the complaining parties that is, a natural person or corporate body, professional organisations, consumer associations and the electricity operator on the other hand.[331] This exercise shall be sanctioned by a report prepared by the Electricity Sector Regulatory Board signed by the two parties. It is oneribes to note that cases of this nature reported to the consumer association by natural persons have nothing to ride home.

Article 6 of the Electricity Law provides that the settlement of a dispute may be settled by the Electricity Sector Regulatory Board. The Board could be seised by an electricity operator and the conditions for such a settlement are laid down by the Board. Similarly, Article 24 of the Water mandates the

[328] Arbitration is advantageous over courts because (i) it is often faster than litigation (ii) arbitral proceedings and an arbitral award are generally non-public, and can be made confidential (iii) in arbitral proceedings the language of arbitration may be chosen, whereas in judicial proceedings the official language of the country of the competent court will automatically be applied (iv) there is little or no room for appeal of an arbitral award which limits the duration of the dispute and any associated liability.

[329] Article 92 of the Electricity Law.

[330] Article 23, Water Law.

[331] Section 5, Electricity Law.

local chiefs to also settle water related litigations through arbitration. It is but obvious that such an exercise must be done in compliance with rules governed by the Arbitration Law, which eventually is the OHADA Uniform Act on Arbiration Law.[332]

5.1.4 Advisory Councils

In the light of facilitating and hearing the rights of consumer complaints the National Advisory Council[333] under the Ministry in charge of Commerce is mandated with such task. The National Consumer Council shall be an advisory body whose mission is;

- To promote the exchange of views between public authorities, organisations protecting the collective interest of consumers and employers organisations.

- To promote cooperation between representatives of consumer interests and delegates of employers organisations on matters relating to the protection of consumers;

- To issue opinions on all draft legislative and regulatory texts likely to affect the consumption of goods and services or to the consumer protection submitted to it by the government.

With the above disposition in place, it there implies that complaints related to electricity and water could be addressed by this Council for the onerib of consumers. Regrettably the oneribesn and functioning of the National Consumer Advisory Council is slow to be effectively operational.

[332] Section 6, Electricity Law.
[333] Article 25, Electricity Law.

5.1.4.1 Appeal Committees

Appeal committees are set up at the level of each Sub-Division to carry out the role of public services through arbitration of disputes arising from consumer protection issues. The oneribesn and functioning of the commission has been done by a Prime Ministerial Order[334]. According to Article 3[335], the Appeals committee has to be made up of a president and members. The president has to be the sub-divisional officer or his representatives. It is made up of three members, namely, the sub-divisional chief of brigade for control and repression of fraud territorially competent; a representative of the consumer protection associations that is registered with the ministry in charge of protection of consumers, chosen by the Divisional Officer (DO), on proposal of the chief of service of control and repression of fraud; a representative of the professionals of the activity/service in question appointed by the sub-divisional officer territorially competent based on a proposal of the chief of service of control and repression of fraud.

As for the functioning of these committees, they come together on the convocation of the president who addresses the convocation alongside with the working documents to the various members before the session's précising the date, time and place. This must be done within 48 hours before the holding of the session. The secretariat is handled by the center for control repression of fraud territorially competent. The president of the committee can also decide to invite other persons to participate in the session but they have only a consultative role based on the areas of competence as to the order of the day.[336]

The procedure for dispute settlement by the Appeals Committee has been provided for in article 6 (1) of the Prime Ministerial order which states that the procedure can start with an amicable arrangements. The consumer and the professional (retailer, the supplier of technology or service provider)

[334] Order No. 119/PM of 10 August 2012.
[335] Article 3 of Order No. 119/PM of 10 August 2012.
[336] Article 4 (2) of Order No. 119/PM of 10 August 2012.

can decide to first of all submit their dispute to an amicable arrangement. In case the quest for amicable settlement fails, the consumer has a delay of 30 days to cease the appeal committee. The consumer ceases the committee by a complaint addressed to the president in which he/she requests the president to annul, cancel or revise the contract and can likely ask for damages.[337] As such, the order limits the competence of the committees only to actions of compensation. Preventive actions seem not to be of their competence since they can only be brought up by consumer associations.

5.2 Judicial Sanctions

There are numerous offence provisions in Cameroon's CSR legislation but reported cases dealing with CSR prosecutions are few. The main reason for this is that offences in violation of CSR are mostly settled out of court with the implementation of administrative sanctions. The administration only reverts to the courts as last resort, when the offender fails to comply with the administrative sanctions imposed. The courts play a very important role in the enforcement of corporate social responsibility and environmental law in general. The disadvantage with the judiciary as a CSR enforcement institution is that court actions most often are engaged when the harm is already done. As a result, most of the decisions of the courts are meant to punish the wrongdoers but at the same time compensate the victim and deter future violators of the law. The courts are usually opened to several forms of sanctions where the accused is found guilty. However, the Environmental Code makes provision for two principal penalties which are fine and imprisonment.

5.2.1 Imprisonment

Section 24 of the Penal Code defines imprisonment as: "*loss of liberty during which the offender shall be obliged to work, subject to any contrary order of the court for reasons to be recorded in the judgement.*"[338] Even though

[337] Article 7 of Order No. 119/PM of 10 August 2012.

[338] Section 24 of Law No. 65/LF/24 of 12/11/1965 and Law No. 67/LF/1 of 12/06/1967 on the Cameroon Penal Code as modified by Law No. 2016/007 of July 12 2016, relating to the Penal Code.

the 2011 Electricity Law and Water Law do not expressly make provision of imprisonment, resort to the Environmental Law[339] makes provision for the penalty of imprisonment as a principal sanction, which varies depending on the gravity of the offence.

These offences and penalties may be classified into two main categories notably, violation and penalty for failure to carry out or improper execution of environmental impact assessment and pollution. Accordingly, the Water Law in its Section 15 (1) makes provision of an imprisonment term as contained in Section 15 (1) of 2 (two) years to 5 (five) years to whoever does not respect the environmental assessment regulations as laid down by the text.

Also worth noting is the fact that the legislator has scaled the penalty of imprisonment in such a way that it leaves the judge with the latitude to use his discretion in administering the sentence. This means that, depending on the facts of the case, the judge may either award the highest or the lowest penalty of imprisonment. Whatever the case, the judge is not allowed to impose imprisonment term that is above the maximum penalty provided by the legislator in the Environmental Code and enabling instruments for that particular offence.

Surprisingly, it seems increasingly clear that the courts in Cameroon are content with the application of the sanction of fine and other accessory penalties to the detriment of imprisonment when the offender involved is a corporate institution, even as the Environmental Code makes provisions for imprisonment. A justification for this is the existence of a panoply of case in this respect, whereas it is difficult to find Cameroonian cases on the violation of CSR where the courts have actually implemented the sanction of imprisonment.

[339] Law No. 96/12 of 5th August 1996 relating to Environmental Management in Cameroon (Environmental Code).

In the case of *SCAN EQUIP v. MINEP*[340], the defendant, a chemical company in Douala which produces oil, grease, paints and dilatants was noted for dumping its waste into nature. In an attempt to make it stop the act, it was warned on several occasions but it refused to heed to the warnings. In 2002, MINEF sued the company in the Court of First Instance in Douala for refusing to stop the pollution. After serious investigation, the court found that they had violated Section 29 of the Environmental Code and were only asked to pay a fine of 2,800,000FCFA according to Section 82 of the Code.[341] No penalty of imprisonment was attached even as there had been repeated warnings. A similar decision was applied in the case of *MINEF v. Cameroon Railway Corporation (CAMRAIL)*.[342] Here again, after finding CAMRAIL guilty of violating section 43(1) of the Environmental Code, the company was only asked to pay a fine of 2,500,000FCFA.[343] This attitude of the courts in Cameroon has left room for several unanswered questions: Do the judges find it comfortable and less stressful imposing only fines? Does the doctrine of corporate personality stand as a major challenge to application of imprisonment?[344] Are the courts in their reluctant attitude to implement the sanction of imprisonment trying to protect the companies? Whatever the case, what stands out clear is the fact that the courts in Cameroon have been reluctant to sanction companies who violate CSR with imprisonment which has only acted as a disincentive to punishment serving as deterrence to violation, probably the reason why CSR violations are on the rise.

This attitude of the courts in Cameroon has left room for several unanswered questions: Do the judges find it comfortable and less stressful imposing only fines? Does the doctrine of corporate personality stand as a major challenge

[340] Case No. 90/TPI/DLA/March 2002 (unreported).

[341] It can be observed that the fine is too small to deter the defendant from repeating the same offence. This renders the polluter pay principle almost an empty slogan because it may be considered to mean "we pollute because we can pay".

[342] Case No. 20/TPI/DLA /12 April 2003 (unreported).

[343] See also *The People & MINEF v. Bernard Brink Co.* Case No. 83/BA/78C/03-04 (Unreported) *&SOTRAMILK v. MINEF*, Case No. o8/CF/BA/1245/02.03 (unreported).

[344] The corporate organic theory seems to shield the management of the companies from their acts. The consequences of these actions are that they can be attributed to the company itself.

to application of imprisonment?[345] Are the courts in their reluctant attitude to implement the sanction of imprisonment trying to protect the companies? Whatever the case, what stands out clear is the fact that the courts in Cameroon have been reluctant to sanction companies who violate CSR with imprisonment which has only acted as a disincentive to punishment serving as deterrence to violation, probably the reason why CSR violations are on the rise.

5.2.2 Criminal Fines

As a general rule, Section 74 of the Cameroon Penal Code provides for the criminal responsibility of corporate bodies. The law provides that corporate bodies shall be criminally responsible for offences committed on their behalf by their organs or representatives. In addition, there is reference to the application of criminal sanctions contained in the Penal Code by the laws on electricity and water[346] in order to complement those already provided by the same texts.

A principal penalty, whose application has found favour in the courts in Cameroon as far as corporate social responsibility is concerned, is criminal fines. The appellation criminal fine is derived from the fact that when the courts apply this sanction, the money is paid into state coffers and precisely the special environmental fund. Fines are pecuniary compensations which an offender pays to the state. They are usually paid in place of an imprisonment term. However, there are instances where the convicted person serves both a term of imprisonment and equally pays a fine. It is mostly for simple offences and misdemeanours that fines are imposed. Where an offender is fined and he isunable to pay the said fine, he would have to serve a term of imprisonment. The provisions of Section 53(2) of the Penal Code are instructive as far as the fine is concerned.[347]

[345] The corporate organic theory seems to shield the management of the companies from their acts. The consequences of these actions are that they can be attributed to the company itself.

[346] Section 17, Water Law.

[347] See generally Section 53(2) of the Penal Code. It provides that: where the offender, after haven been in custody awaiting trial, is sentenced to a fine only, the court may relief him wholly or in part of the said debt.

Concerning the water sector, Section 261 of the Penal Code[348] states that whoever by his operations "pollutes any drinkable water liable to be used by another..." shall be punished with imprisonment for from 15 (fifteen) days to 6 (six) months, or with fine of from CFAF 5000 (five thousand) to CFAF 1,000,000 (one million), or with such imprisonment and fine. In addition, Section 15 (1) of the Water Law oneribes a fine of CFAF 5 million (5,000,000) to 10 million (1,000,000) CFACF to whoever does not respectct environmental assessment norms as laid down by text.

Section 18 (b) provides for principal penalties as follows: for corporate bodies; Dissolution, temporary or final closure, fines. Section 19 (b) provides accessory penalties for corporate bodies as follows: ban, for a specifies period of time, on the direct or indirect exercise of any or all of its activities; placement under judicial supervision for a specified period of time; closure for a specified period of time of establishments or branches having served in the commission of offences; publication or media broadcast of the judgment; any other accessory penalties provided for by special instruments.

Section 20 talks about preventive measures for corporate bodies: ban on exercise of activity for a specified period of time; confiscation; placement under judicial supervision for a specified period of time. The penal code further provides for dissolution[349] as a capital punishment against corporate bodies. Dissolution may be passed against a corporate body that has acted in violation of its object clause and the judgment on the dissolution of a corporate body shall refer such corporate body to the competent court for winding up at the instance of the Legal Department.

Criminal sanctions are also meted out in case wrongful information is given to competent authorities or any structure concerned with consumer protection

[348] Law No. 2016/007 of 12 July 2016
[349] Section 25 (2), Penal Code.

issues or consumer protection organisations. Article 32 (1) punishes with imprisonment of six (6) months to two (2) years and a fine of two hundred and one thousand (201,000) to one million (1,000,000) FCFA or one of these two penalties for whosoever provides incorrect information on the quality of technology, goods or services that are supplied or offered to the consumer.[350] Art. 32 (2) anyone who gives false information is subject to the penalties provided for in paragraph 1 above. Art. 33, without prejudice to the criminal liability of managers or employees of companies, sales, supply or service, technology or goods, legal persons can be sentenced to double the fines provided for in section 32, if the offences committed by their officers or employees were during or in the exercise of their function within the said structures.

Cases of CSR violation where the courts have applied the sanction of criminal fines abound.

In the case of *SCAN EQUIP* (supra), after establishing that the defendant company violated Section 29 of the Environmental Code, the company was fined 2,800,000FCFA according to Section 82 of the Code. A similar decision was applied in the case of *MINEF v. Cameroon Railway Corporation (CAMRAIL)* (supra).[351] Fines of this nature are relatively small for such companies, which explain why the companies paid the fine with little stress. This again questions the desire of the courts to actually deter others from exhibiting similar conducts.

---

[350] Article 32 (1), 2011, Legal Framework on Consumer Protection.

[351] In that case, CAMRAIL'S coaches derailed and fell at Badjob, 15km from Esseka on the 1st of February 2003. The hydrocarbons that came out from the coaches polluted the land on which they stood. After a visit of MINEF's workers to the venue, a complaint letter No. B252/SG of 10th July 2003 was sent to the Prime Minister by MINEF. He responded quickly by saying that the environmental Code should be applied. MINEF then entered into an agreement with the latter to clean the affected area. But it was discovered later that the agreement had not been respected. The matter was then sent to court where CAMRAIL was found guilty of violating Section 43(1) of the Environmental Code and the company was asked to pay a fine of 2,500,000FCFA. A similar position was held in *The People & MINEF v. Bernard Brink Co* Case No. 83/BA/78C/03-04, (unreported). See also *SOTRAMILK v. MINEF*, Case No. 08/CF/BA/1245/02.03, (unreported).

5.2.3 Tort of Negligence

The principle of negligence holds a person who does any act without exercising reasonable care liable for damages to all those it is reasonable to say he had in contemplation while doing the act or omission in question, for any damage it is reasonable to say he should foresee as arising from his conduct. It has three vital ingredients: duty of care, breach of duty and consequential damage. Generally, for a claimant to succeed in an action for negligence he must not only show that the defendant owed him a duty of care but also that the defendant is in breach of the duty. This he has to do by showing that the defendant did not exercise reasonable care in the matter that is in issue as a result of which he has suffered the damage sought to be redressed.[352]

In relation to consumer protection, the problem posed by the doctrine of privity of contract can be overcome through the law of tort. A gratuitous one or an innocent bystander who suffers injury, loss or damage as a result of a defective product or the negligent act of another can sue in negligence without being weighed down by the requirement of contractual relationship. The tort of negligence, however, has its limitations which constitute serious difficulty in consumer protection. For example, liability arises only where the plaintiff can prove fault against the defendant, and he cannot recover for pure economic loss unaccompanied by physical injury to person or property. He must prove the particular act or omission of the defendant that amounts to a breach of duty of care, and will fail if there is no causal link between his injury, loss or damage and the act of the defendant complained of. This makes the tort of negligence an appropriate head of claim for consumers of electricity for cases where personal injury or damage to property is caused by defective product supplied by a service provider or his faulty operational equipment.

[352] On this, see, F. O. Ukwueze, "Unfair Terms in Consumer Contracts in Nigeria: The Need for Stricter Statutory Control" in F. N. Monye (ed), (2007) Consumer *Journal*, Vol. 3 pp. 41 – 57.

In Cameroon, there is an incessant outcry of consumers of electricity for damage caused to their personal consumables goods due to interrupted power failure caused probably their defective equipments and appliances. Regretabbly, because of huge financial costs to seise the courts with cases scare the aggrieved consumers from taking legal actions.

5.2.4 Other Penalties

Besides the imposition of the principal penalties of loss of liberty and fine, the trial court may impose some other secondary or accessory penalties. In the case where these secondary penalties are attached to the principal penalties, they usually take effect after service of the principal penalty. Most often, it is presumed that secondary penalties only act as reinforcement to the principal penalties of imprisonment and fine. In the case of *Cameroon Railway Corporation (CAMRAIL)* (supra), the court, after establishing that CAMRAIL was guilty of violating Section 43(1) of the Environmental Code, obliged the company to pay a fine of 2,500,000FCFA in addition to an order to clean and rehabilitate the affected land. The attachment of the order obliging the company to clean and rehabilitate the affected land was a demonstration of recognition by the courts of the curative corporate social responsibility. Here, the trial court went further to attach other sanctions to the fine. Further judicial support to the use of secondary/ accessory sanctions was demonstrated in the case of *The People & MINEF v. Bernard Brink Co*. (supra). After attaching guilt to the defendant, the Court of First Instance in Bamenda, Cameroon attached an order stopping defendant from continuing the disposition of effluent into the stream to the fine of 5,000,000 F CFA.[353]

From the above, it is evident that the sanctions previewed by the Cameroonian legislator against violators of CSR are not stringent enough to effectively deter corporate bodies from executing activities that contribute to climate

[353] For further judicial support to this, see *SOTRAMILK v. MINEF* Case No. 08/CF/BA/1245/02.03, (unreported).

change. The logical interpretation of this is that companies find it cost effective to violate the CSR regulations and pay than incur the cost of toeing the line drawn by CSR legislation. In addition to this, administrative desire to continuously reap the economic benefits that MNCs bring and the fear of losing the companies have prioritised the use of out of court settlements of fines and compromise to court prosecution.

Furthermore, even when few cases are referred to the courts, the lack of follow-up is another drawback with CSR cases because even when judgements are handed down there is hardly any follow up to guarantee implementation. This is what obtained in the *SOTRAMILK v. MINEF'scase*.[354] The judge stated that the respondent should rehabilitate the polluted area under the supervision of the appellant without taking steps such as a visit to the *locus in quo* to ensure that the judgement was executed. It is logical that if the judge visits the *locus in quo* after the supposed exercise, this would compel respondents to always do what the judgement obliged them to do. But, understanding that most judges do not visit the site, respondents hardly effectively comply with the court's instructions and this renders the deterrent effect of an otherwise severe judgement simply diluted.

5.3 Conclusion

The concept of having CSR policies and practices by companies in Cameroon is still relatively new and slow in its implementation. However, ENEO has been identified as the electricity company in Cameroon in order to assess the

[354] In this case, the defendant a yoghurt producing company located at mile 3 Nkwen, Bamenda, had been systematically discharging industrial waste into a stream close to it. This caused pollution of the water, making it unfit for drinking. The defendant also burnt empty plastic bottles of yoghurt, leading to air pollution and destruction of the land on which they were burnt contrary to Section 29 of the Environmental Code. Judgement was passed in favour of the plaintiff in the Bamenda Court of First Instance. The court applied just the accessory penalty of prohibitory injunction restraining the respondent from further discharging milky waste or industrial sewage into the stream. A mandatory injunction was also applied, requiring the respondent to rehabilitate the polluted areas near the factory under the strict supervision of the appellant in conformity with the CSR curative responsibility of rehabilitation or restoration of the degraded environment.

level of implantation of their corporate environmental through their activities and projects to help the local communities from suffering from environmental problems of varied nature. However, this paper argues that ENEO's CER policies are targeted towards urban areas that do not desperately need the measures as much as the societies where their equipments are located. Most of the people especially in the rural areas surrounding do not have pipe borne water to avoid drinking contaminated water; schools to educate the community on the effect of the dams; no good roads to ensure safe transportation etc. Conversly, ENEO seems to be a great environmental concern to the local communities and the country at large.

If one were to judge from the perspective of the quantum of regulations and institutions, it would be agreed that as a country, Cameroon has fared reasonably well in corporate social responsibility. Unfortunately, this effort, laudable as it may be, has taken place within the inadequate ambit of weak and insufficiently articulated CSR policy – a situation that calls for rectification. Even with the existing current legislations on CSR, there are still lacunae. This paper has sufficiently demonstrated the legislative efforts through the sanctions aimed at enforcing corporate social responsibility in Cameroon. The efforts made in this respect are enormous: prescription of specific conducts for companies, legislative incrimination of certain conducts, provision of extra judicial sanctions (imposition of fines, rehabilitation, a stop to certain conduct and suspension and withdrawal of authorisation) and the use of the courts in the enforcement of judicial sanctions. However, as far as any careful observer can see, these sanctions are yet to be satisfactory, and the reasons are not far-fetched.

It is therefore our humble submission that if environmental policies have to be effectively brought to a supportable level by regulating the activities of water corporations through corporate social responsibility, environmental policy and law reforms as well as institutional reforms must be given place of pride. The former requires amongst other things; supplementation of the legislative framework of environmental control with the use of market instruments such as heavy taxes on environmentally-damaging goods and subsidies on new clean technology, the introduction of draconian sanctions in the environmental laws and policies so that they can effectively deter violations, institution of a proper framework law in the right sense of the expression governing environmental aspects of corporate social responsibility in Cameroon or alternatively, the 1996 Environmental Law of Cameroon should clearly and expressly encapsulate environmental aspects of corporate social responsibility and international customary law standards. As for the latter, we suggest that environmental litigations should be simplified and the courts be made more liberal on the issue of *locus standi* so that meritorious cases can be readily entertained, a reduction in corporation's ability to lobby, industries in Cameroon should be advised, encouraged and forced, where necessary, to adapt production practices that minimise damage to the environment and education of the people on their legal rights in the area of environmental litigation.

SELECTED BIBLIOGRAPHY

I. Books

- Achoundong G, *Le Bois Sacre de la Chefferie Bafou*, (Yaounde, Herbier National, 1990.
- Alan E. Boyle and Michael R. Anderson, *Human Rights Approaches to Environmental Protection*,Oxford, OUP, 1996.
- Carroll A. and Buchholtz A., *Business and Society: Ethics and Stakeholder Management*, Mason, OH: Thomson South-Western, 2003.
- Chi Augustine, *Co-management of Forest in Cameroon: The Compatibility of Government Policies with Indigenous Practices*, University of Twente,, Drienerveld, 1999.
- Christopher F. Tamasang & Sylvain N. Atanga, Environmental Impact Assessment under Cameroonian Law, In Environmental Law and Policy in Cameroon –Towards making Africa the Tree of Life, (Oliver C. Ruppel Emmanuel D. Kam Yogo [eds./dir.) Germany, Nomos Verlagsgesellschaft, 2018.
- Goodpaster, Kenneth E., *Conscience and Corporate Culture*, Malden, Massachusetts: Blackwell Publishing, 2007.
- Hillary, R, *Environmental Management Standards, what do SMEs think?* In ISO 14001 and Beyond, Sheldon C (ed.), Greenleaf, Sheffield, 1977.
- Hunter, D., Saizman, J., Zaelke, D., *International Environmental Law and Policy*, New York, Foundation Press, 1998.
- James A. Graff, *Human Rights, Peoples, and the Right to Self-Determination, in Group Rights*, Judith Baker ed., 1994.

- Kiss, A., Shelton, D., *International Environmental Law* (3rd ed., New York, Transnational Publishers, 2004.
- Leite and Weidman, *A Survey of Corruption Issues in the Mining & Mineral Sector*. England:International Institute for Environment and Development, 2001.
- Mazurkiewicz P, *Corporate Environmental Responsibility: Is a common CSR framework possible*, DevComm-SDO, World Bank, 2004.
- Michel Nyoth Hiol, Le Droit Camerounais de l'Energie, In Environmental Law and Policy in Cameroon –Towards making –Towards making Africa the Tree of Life, (Oliver C. Ruppel Emmanuel D. Kam Yogo [eds./dir.) Germany, Nomos Verlagsgesellschaft, 2018.
- Norrington-Davies G. "Climate Change Financing and Aid Effectiveness: Cameroon Case Study", (2011), OECD.
- Ntiamoa-Baidu, Y. "Indigenous vs. Introduced Biodiversity Conservation Strategies: The case of protected areas systems in Ghana", (1995), African Biodiversity Series, Number I, May 1995, 1-11, Washington: The Biodiversity Support Program.
- Rossouw, D., *Business Ethics in Africa*, 2nd ed., Cape Town: Oxford University Press 2002.
- Shari, B & Barrie H. Transparency and Accountability in Africa's Extractive Industries, National Democratic Institute for International Affairs (NDI), 2007.
- Tamasang Christopher, Environmental Impact Assessment under Cameeroonian Law in *Environmental Law and policy in Cameroon – Towards making Africa the Tree of Life* (Oliver C. Ruppel Emmanuel D. Kam Yogo [eds./dir.) Germany, Nomos Verlagsgesellschaft, 2018.
- Welford R. (2000), *Corporate Environmental Responsibility 3: Towards Sustainable Development*, Earthscan, London, cited in Welford, R (2003).

II. Articles/Journals

- Alao J. S. and Shuaibu, R. B., (2013) "Agroforestry Practices and Concepts in Sustainable Land use Systems in Nigeria", *Journal of Horticulture and Forestry*, Vol. 5(10).
- Cameron, J., and Abouchar, J,(1991)"The Precautionary Principle: A Fundamental Principle of Law and Policy for the Protection of the Global Environment",14 B.C. *International & Comparative Law Review* 1, 2.
- Deval Desai, (2009) "Courting" Legitimacy: Democratic Agency and the Justiciability of Economic and Social Rights, *Interdisciplinary Journal of Human Rights Law*.
- Edwin Mujih, (2004) "The Regulation of Multinational Corporations operating in Developing Countries: A Case Study of the Chad-Cameroon Pipeline Project, Social Responsibility: *An International Journal*.
- Emeka O., Adedoyin, R., &Adeola D. (2008) "Environmental Issues and Corporate Social Responsibility. The Nigerian Experience", *Kamla-Raj Journal of Human Ecology*, 23(2).
- F. O. Ukwueze, (2007) "Unfair Terms in Consumer Contracts in Nigeria: The Need for Stricter Statutory Control" in F. N. Monye (ed), Consumer *Journal*, Vol. 3.
- Gundling L., (1990) "The Status in International Law of the Principle of Precautionary Action, 5 International Journal of Estuarine and Coastal Law, 23, 26.
- Gandhiv Kafle,(2011)"An Overview of Shifting Cultivation with Reference to Nepal", *International Journal of Biodiversity and Conservation*, Vol. 3(5).
- Kaba Eric Tah, (2012)"The African Conservation Delima: Ancient Tradition vs. Modern Greed, in Wildlife Justice, African Traditions and Wildlife Conservation", *Bilingual Wildlife Law Enforcement Journal*, N0 008, 1-12.

- Kimerling J. (1994) “Environmental Justice or Business as Usual? The Case of Environmental Monitoring and Audit of Texaco’s Amazon Oil Fields”, 7 *Harvard Human Rights Journal.*
- Lipman Z. and Roots L.(1995) “Protecting the Environment through Criminal Sanctions: The Environmental Offences and Penalties Act 1989 (NSW)” 12 *Environment and Planning Law Journal.*
- Lodhia S., (2005) “Legitimacy Motives for World Wide Web (www) Environmental Reporting: An Exploratory Study into Present Practices in the Australian Minerals Industry”, *Journal of Accounting and Finance*, 4.
- Marquis, C., Glynn, M. A. and Davis, G. F. “Community Isomorphism and Corporate Social Action”, (2007), *Academy of Management Review*, 32, 3.
- Munang T., Rivington M., Bellocchi G., Azam-Ali S., Colls J., (2008)“Effects of Climate Change on Crop Production in Cameroon”, (2008), *Climate Research*, 36.
- Norrington-Davies G. (2011), “Climate Change Financing and Aid Effectiveness: Cameroon Case Study”, OECD, available at http://www.oecd.org/dac/environment-development/48458474.
- Richard N. Kiwanuka, (1988) “The Meaning of ‘People’ in the African Charter of Human and Peoples’ Rights”, 82 *American Journal of International Law.*
- Rim-Rukeh A., Irerhievwie G., Agbozu I.E., (2013) “Traditional Beliefs and Conservation of Natural Resources: Evidences from selected communities in Delta State, Nigeria”, *International Journal of Biodiversity and Conservation*, Vol. 5(7).
- YongD.,(2013) “Agriculture and Climate Change in Cameroon: An Assessment of Impacts and Adaptation Options,” *Journal of Science, Technology, Innovation and Development*, Vol.5, 1.

III. Reviews/Reports/Papers

- Dias A., Human Rights, Environment and Development: with Special Emphasis on Corporate Accountability, (2000), Human Development Report, Background Paper.
- Eyebe A., Simeon A. E., Angu K. A., and Endamana D., (2012), "Integrating Biodiversity Conservation into National Development Policy: A Case Study of Cameroon," IIED Poverty and Conservation Learning Group Discussion Paper, No. 09.
- E. V. K. Fitzgerald, 'Regulating Large International Firms' UNRISD Programme on Technology, Business and society, Paper No. 5, November 2001.
- European Commission (2001), Promoting a European Framework for Corporate Social Responsibility, *Green Paper*.
- Friedman M., "The Social Responsibility of Business is to Increase its Profits", (1970), *The New York Times Magazine*, Section 6.
- Molua E. & Lambi C., "The Economic Impact of Climate Change on Agriculture in Cameroon", (2006), *CEEPA Discussion Paper* No. 17, CEEPA, University of Pretoria.
- R. Jenkins, 'Corporate Code of conduct: self-regulation in a Global Economy', UNRISD Programme on Technology, Business and Society. Paper No. 2. April 2001.
- Sadler B. (1996), *Environmental Assessment in a Changing World: Evaluating Practice to Improve Performance*. International Study of the Effectiveness of Environmental Assessment. Final Report. Canadian Environmental Assessment Agency, International Association for Impact Assessment, UNCED (1992) & Agenda 21.
- Youssaou M. (2011). *Les Question Environnementaux sur la Désertification au Cameroun*. Paper presented at the workshop on Statistics of the Environment, Yaoundé, 5-9 December.

IV. Theses/Dissertations

- Alemagi Dieudonne, *Towards a Comprehensive Strategy for the Effective and Efficient Management of Industrial Pollution along the Atlantic Coast of Cameroon*, (Ph.D Thesis, Brandenburg University of Technology Cottbus 2006) (Unpublished).
- Cyprian Mbou Monoji, Corporate Environmental Governance in Cameroon: A Legal Perspective, (Ph.D Thesis, University of Dschang 2020). (Unpublished).
- Goosen, Xenia, Institutionalising Ethics in Organisations: The role of mentorship, (M.Phil Thesis, Rand Afrikaans University, South Africa 2004).
- Nguefack Donzeu Gael, La Responsabilite Sociale des Entreprises dans l'Espace OHADA, (Ph.D Thesis, University of Dschang, 2020). (Unpublished).
- Nukpezah Daniel, Corporate Environmental Governance in Ghana: Studies on Industrial Level Environmental Performance in Manufacturing and Mining, (PhD Thesis, Brandenburg University of Technology, Cottbus 2010). (Unpublished).
- Tamasang, C. F, Community Forest Management Entities as Effective tool for Local Level Participation under Cameroonian Law: A Case Study of Kilum/Ijim Mountain Forest, (Ph.D Thesis, University of Yaoundé II, Soa 2008), (Unpublished).

V. Links

- http://dx.doi.org/10.3152/147154600781767592
- http://www.academicjournals.org/IJBC
- http://www.academicjournals.org/ijbc
- http://www.cbd.int/doc/world/cm/cm- nbsap- v2- en.pdf
- http://www.cbd.int/doc/world/cm/cm- nr- 05- fr.pdf

- http://www.iied.org/mmsd/mmsd_pdfs/marshall_corruption.pdf
- http://www.nomos-elibrary.de.agb
- http://www.reason.com/news/show/32239.html
- https://www.ceaa.gc.ca/Content/2/B/7/2B7834CA-7D9A-410B-A4ED-FF78AB625BDB/iaia8_e.pd
- https://www.fig.net/resources/publications/figpub/pub36/chapters/chapter_9.pdf
- www.agulhas.co.uk
- www.bsr.org
- www.scape.org